BASS FRETBOARD ATLAS

GET A BETTER GRIP ON NECK NAVIGATION!

BY JOE CHARUPAKORN

T0087272

ISBN 978-1-4950-8036-4

HAL•LEONARD®
7777 W. BLUEMOUND RD. P.O. BOX 13819 MILWAUKEE, WI 53213

In Australia Contact:
Hal Leonard Australia Pty. Ltd.
4 Lentara Court
Cheltenham, Victoria, 3192 Australia
Email: ausadmin@halleonard.com.au

Visit Hal Leonard Online at
www.halleonard.com

TABLE OF CONTENTS

INTRODUCTION

Bass Fretboard Atlas is a collection of roadmaps for the most important scales and arpeggios (up to seventh chords). The material is presented in all 12 keys using 17-fret neck diagrams with color-coded displays of the most common fingerings. When fingerings share common notes, the colors will overlap. No music reading or understanding of music theory is required.

Mastering the bass neck has always been a challenge, even for very experienced players. There are several obstacles that make learning the fretboard especially difficult. On the bass, a note can be played in up to four different places, unlike many other instruments, where each note has only one location.

The diagrams in *Bass Fretboard Atlas* will help you quickly internalize and memorize scales and arpeggios that may have previously seemed impossible to grasp. You'll be able to easily see and understand how scale and arpeggio shapes are laid out, and how they connect and overlap across the neck. As an added benefit, once you can see a shape in your mind's eye, you've got all 12 keys covered—just move the shape to start on a different fret, depending on the key you want.

ABOUT THE AUTHOR

New York City native Joe Charupakorn is a guitarist, editor, and best-selling author. He has written over 25 instructional books for Hal Leonard. His books are available worldwide and have been translated into many languages.

Visit him on the web at *joecharupakorn.com*.

HOW TO USE THIS BOOK

A great strategy for getting the most out of *Bass Fretboard Atlas* is to take one shape and work with it for a while in one key until it feels comfortable. For memorizing scales, first take into account how many notes are on each string and how far apart the notes are in the shape—the distance from one note to the next will, in most cases, be only a fret or two away. (In the case of pentatonic scales, sometimes they are three frets apart). As you become familiar with a scale shape, add in an adjacent shape in the same key. Once you can see both shapes independently and also as pieces of a bigger puzzle, then practice going back and forth between the two. There are countless ways to put the scale shapes to use. For example, you can run the scales straight up and down, improvise with them, or sight-read, using the shapes as a reference. Do this in all 12 keys.

For internalizing arpeggio shapes, first take some time to get a mental picture of the arpeggio's shape. After committing it to memory, practice using it in real-life contexts. Power chord arpeggios are great for rock and pop where root, 5th, and octave bass figures are commonplace. Triad arpeggios are the backbone of virtually any style of music and fall into the "must-know" category. Triads with added notes and seventh chord arpeggios are essential for creating effective, jazzy walking basslines as well as being a harmonically strong soloist.

Beyond the Fingering

For each diagram, every tone of the specific scale or arpeggio is circled, but only the most common shapes are displayed with color codes. This is just a starting point—you shouldn't feel "locked-in" to any of the shapes presented. Feel free to experiment and create shapes that you might find more suitable for specific applications. Because they all interconnect, the idea is that ultimately you'll see the bass neck as one unit.

NOTATION CONVENTIONS IN THIS BOOK

Any note with an *accidental*—a sharp or flat—can be spelled either as a sharp or flat version of the note. In this book, both the sharp and flat versions of every note (*enharmonic equivalents*) are displayed on the fretboard diagrams. The specific accidentals used in the "proper" spelling of a scale or an arpeggio will generally depend on the context.

For example, here is the proper spelling of the G major scale:

G A B C D E F♯ G

And here is an incorrect spelling of the G major scale:

G A B C D E G♭ G

F♯ is the same note as G♭, and, in our diagrams, any note location with that pitch is represented by F♯/G♭ on the fretboard. However, the correct spelling of the G major scale is the one with F♯ because this spelling lets us represent every letter in the music alphabet. In the spelling with G♭, there are no Fs of any kind and two kinds of Gs—a G♭ and a G.

In the headings above the diagrams throughout the book, only the most commonly accepted spellings of the specific scales or chords are displayed.

Exceptions to the Rule

In some cases, it's more practical to suspend the rigidity of the rules and go with a more familiar, if technically "wrong" spelling. This is particularly common in cases involving scales and arpeggios that have double sharps (✕) and double flats (𝄫) in their proper spelling.

The fretboard diagrams in *Bass Fretboard Atlas* do not include double sharps (✕) or double flats (𝄫), or less common accidentals such as F♭, C♭, etc. However, the proper spellings of scales and arpeggios are listed in the headings above the diagrams throughout the book.

For example, the proper spelling of B Lydian ♯2 is:

B C✕ D♯ E♯ F♯ G♯ A♯

While C✕ is enharmonically the same note as D, the dots representing the C✕ notes will be on the fretboard diagram's D notes. Likewise, while E♯ is enharmonically the same note as F, the dots representing the E♯ notes will be on the fretboard diagram's F notes.

If this is all a little confusing, the good news is that, even without any of this information, you'll be able to play any of the scales or arpeggios in any key as long as you can follow the diagrams.

SCALES

THE MAJOR SCALE AND ITS MODES

C IONIAN

C–D–E–F–G–A–B

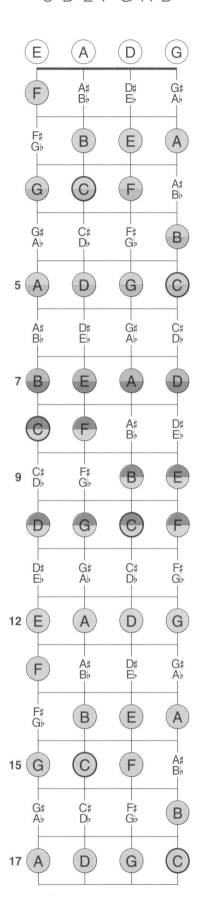

C#/Db IONIAN

C#–D#–E#–F#–G#–A#–B#
Db–Eb–F–Gb–Ab–Bb–C

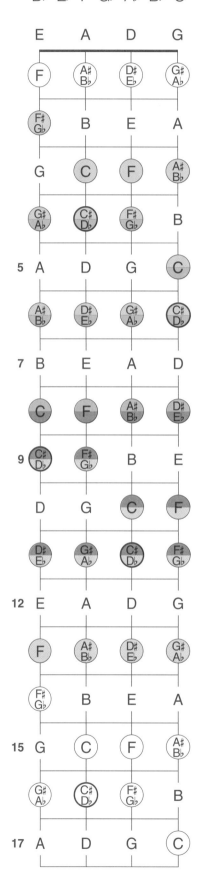

D IONIAN

D–E–F#–G–A–B–C#

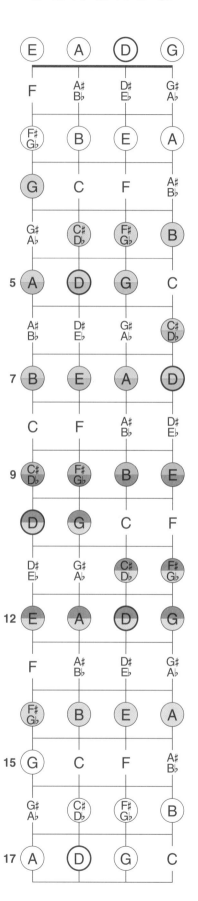

E♭ IONIAN

E♭–F–G–A♭–B♭–C–D

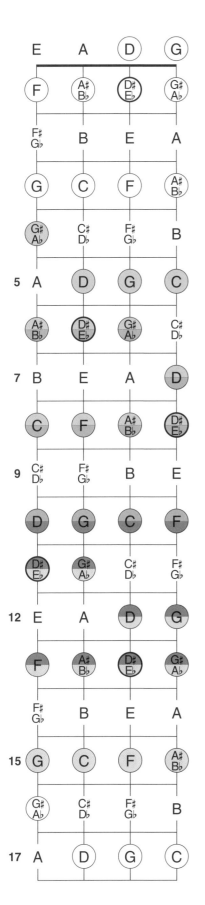

E IONIAN

E–F#–G#–A–B–C#–D#

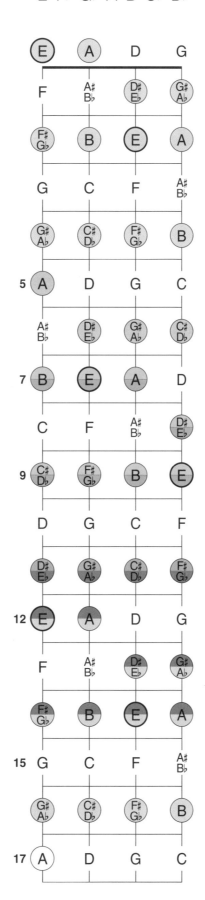

F IONIAN

F–G–A–B♭–C–D–E

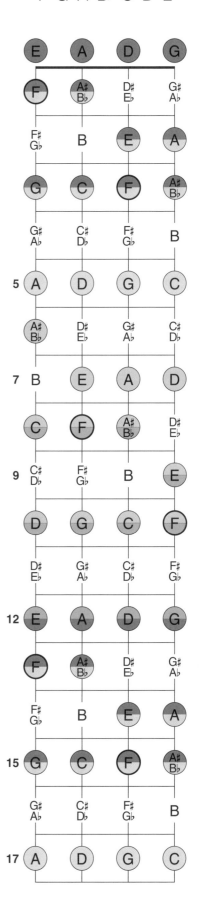

9

F#/G♭ IONIAN

F#–G#–A#–B–C#–D#–E#
G♭–A♭–B♭–C♭–D♭–E♭–F

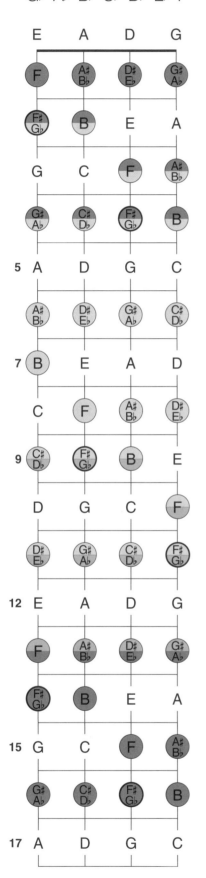

G IONIAN

G–A–B–C–D–E–F#

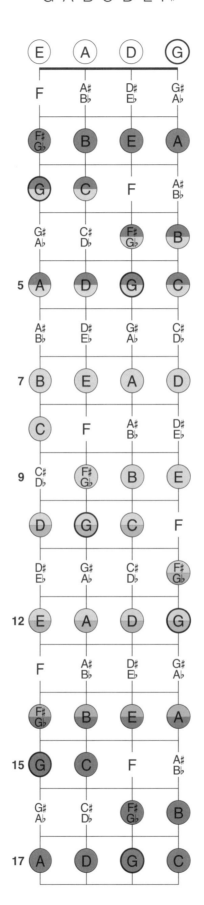

A♭ IONIAN

A♭–B♭–C–D♭–E♭–F–G

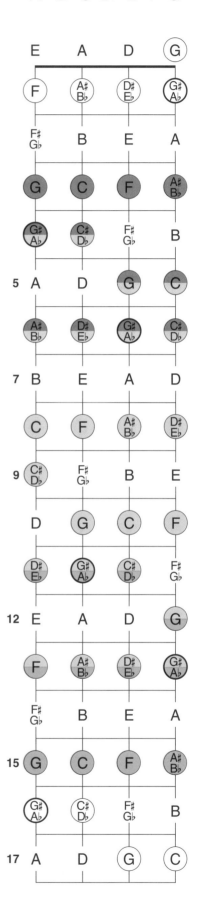

A IONIAN

A–B–C♯–D–E–F♯–G♯

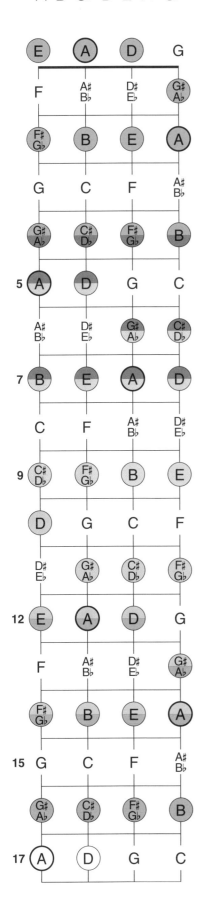

B♭ IONIAN

B♭–C–D–E♭–F–G–A

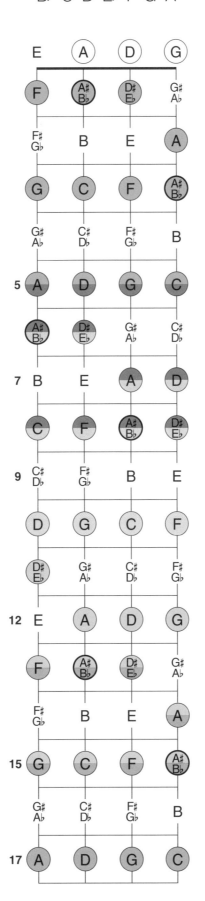

B IONIAN

B–C♯–D♯–E–F♯–G♯–A♯

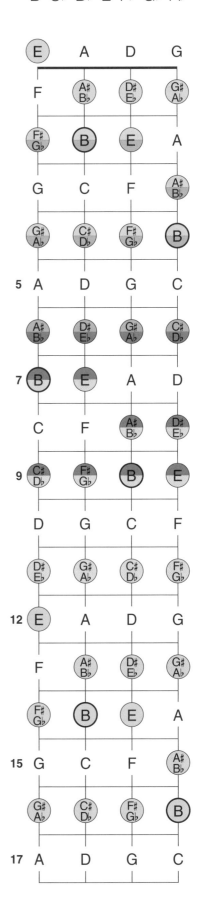

C DORIAN

C–D–E♭–F–G–A–B♭

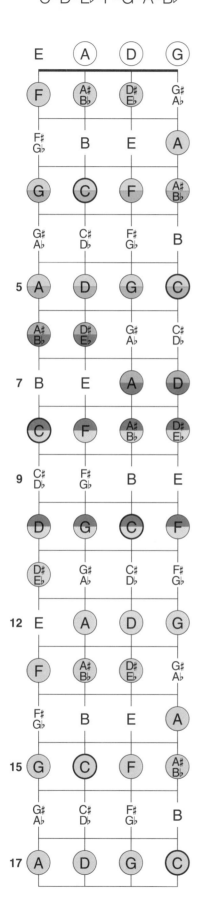

C♯ DORIAN

C♯–D♯–E–F♯–G♯–A♯–B

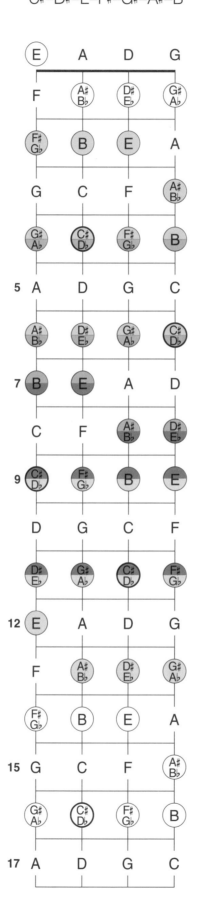

D DORIAN

D–E–F–G–A–B–C

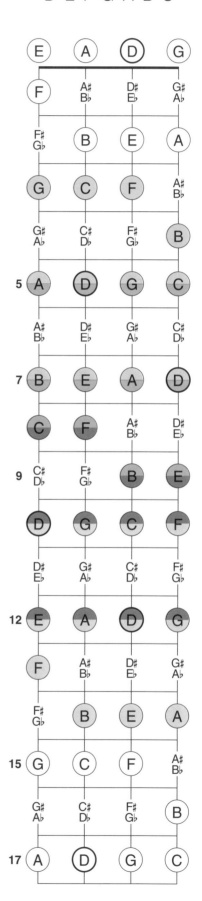

E♭ DORIAN

E♭–F–G♭–A♭–B♭–C–D♭

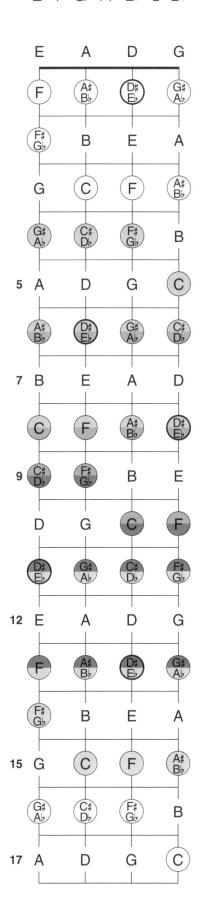

E DORIAN

E–F#–G–A–B–C#–D

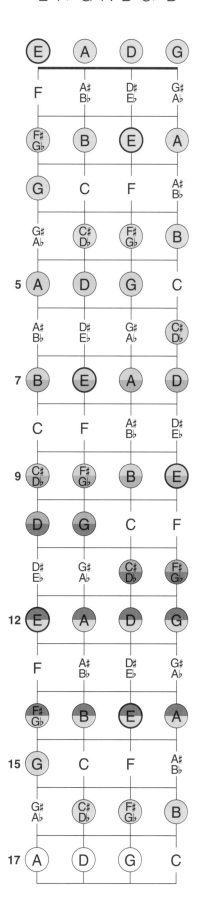

F DORIAN

F–G–A♭–B♭–C–D–E♭

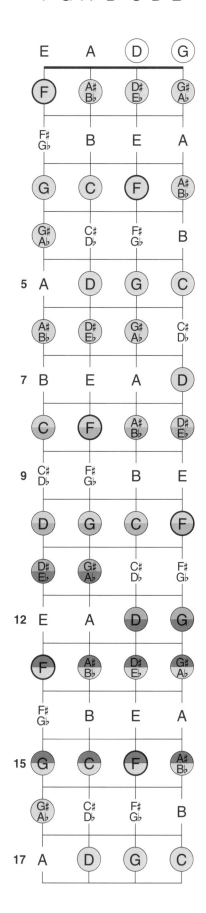

F# DORIAN

F#–G#–A–B–C#–D#–E

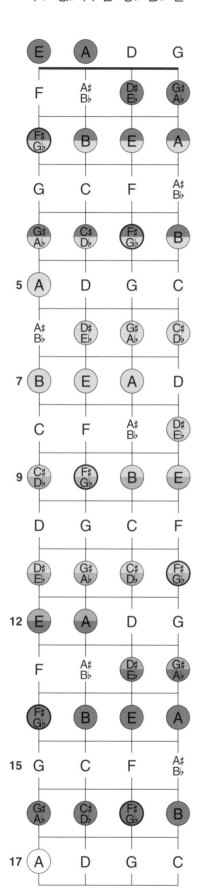

G DORIAN

G–A–Bb–C–D–E–F

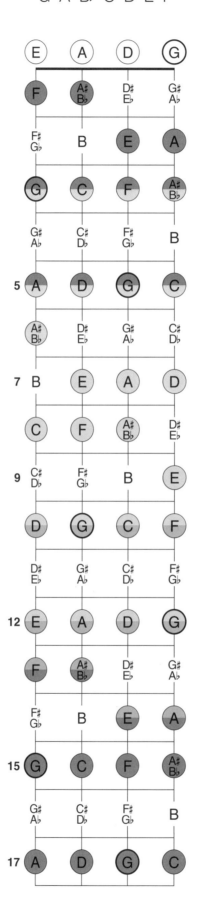

Ab DORIAN

Ab–Bb–Cb–Db–Eb–F–Gb

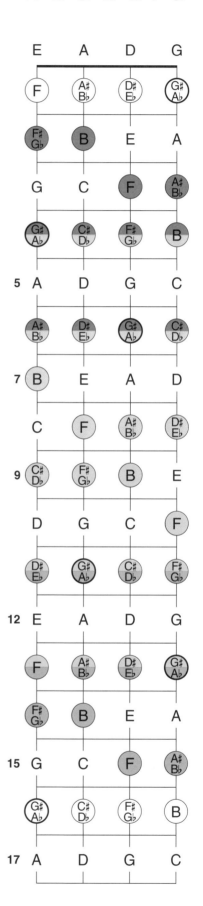

A DORIAN

A–B–C–D–E–F#–G

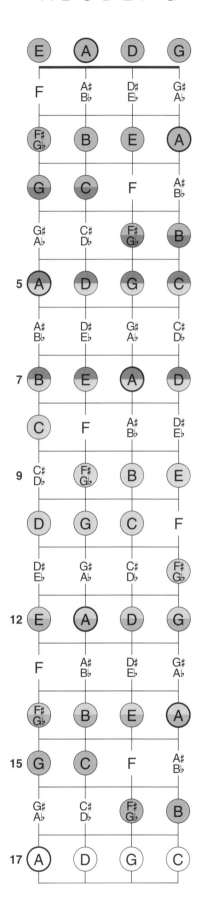

B♭ DORIAN

B♭–C–D♭–E♭–F–G–A♭

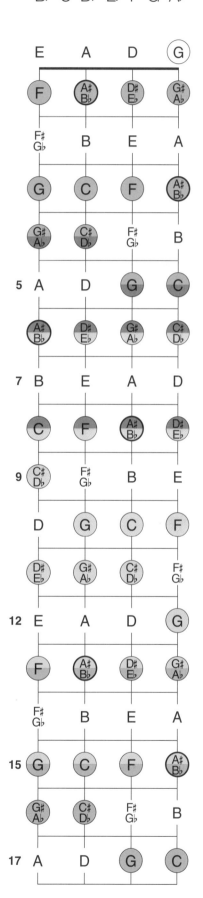

B DORIAN

B–C#–D–E–F#–G#–A

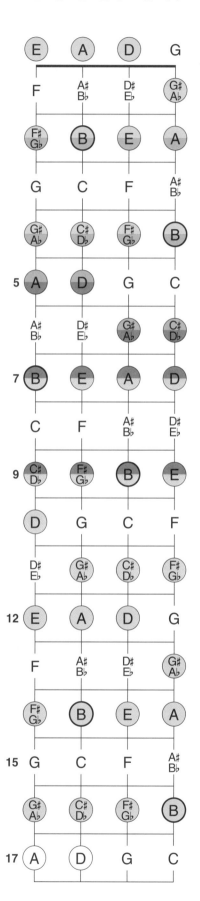

C PHRYGIAN

C–D♭–E♭–F–G–A♭–B♭

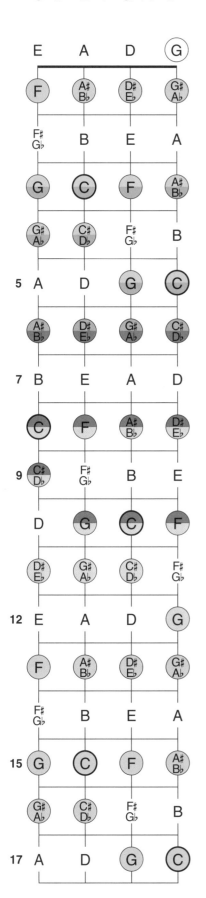

C♯ PHRYGIAN

C♯–D–E–F♯–G♯–A–B

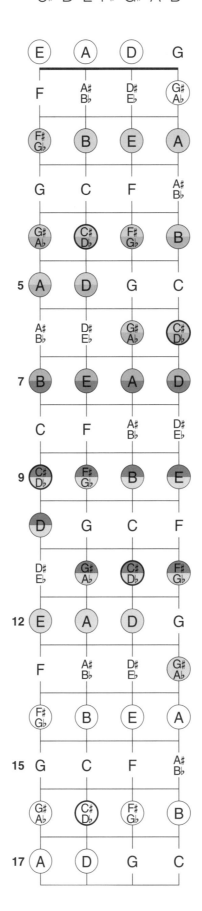

D PHRYGIAN

D–E♭–F–G–A–B♭–C

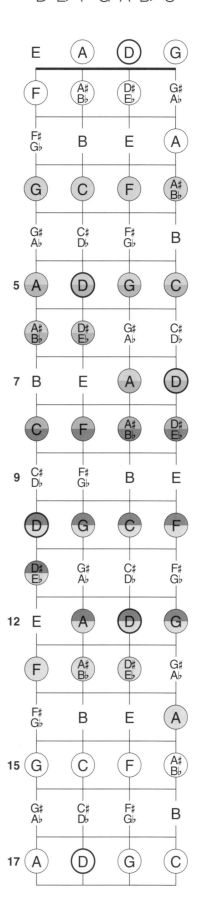

D♯ PHRYGIAN

D♯–E–F♯–G♯–A♯–B–C♯

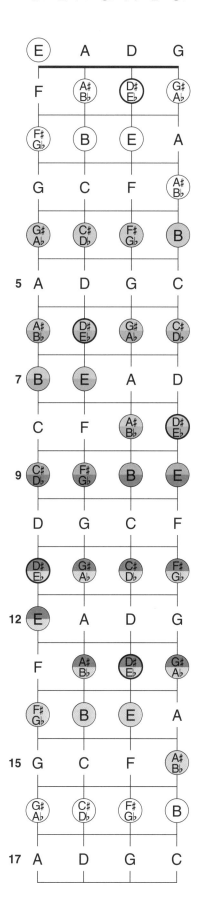

E PHRYGIAN

E–F–G–A–B–C–D

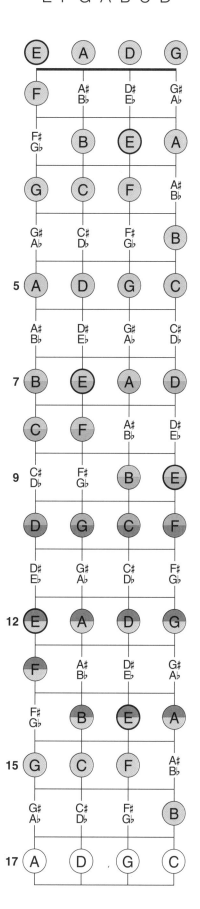

F PHRYGIAN

F–G♭–A♭–B♭–C–D♭–E♭

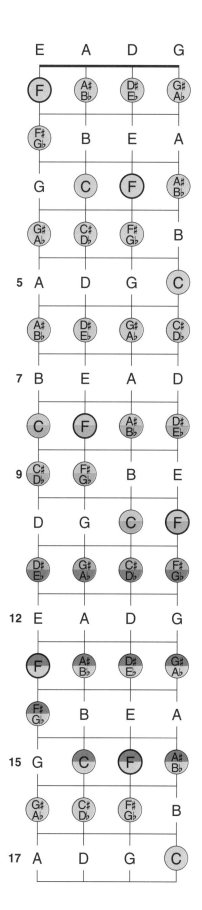

17

F# PHRYGIAN

F#–G–A–B–C#–D–E

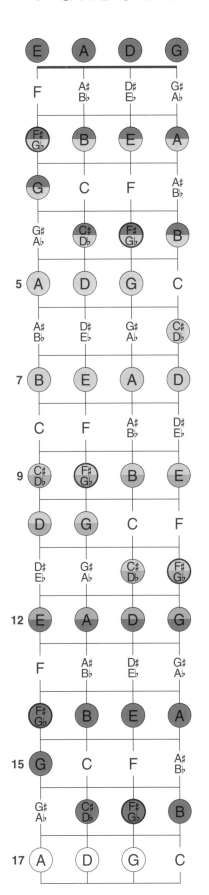

G PHRYGIAN

G–Ab–Bb–C–D–Eb–F

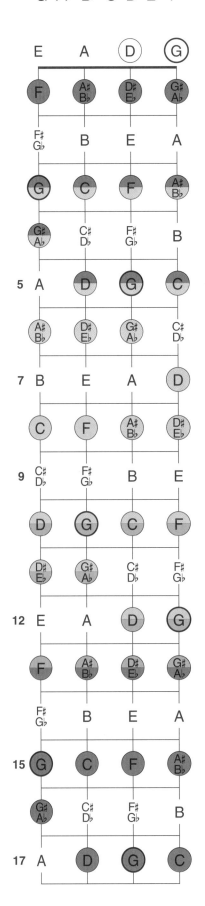

G# PHRYGIAN

G#–A–B–C#–D#–E–F#

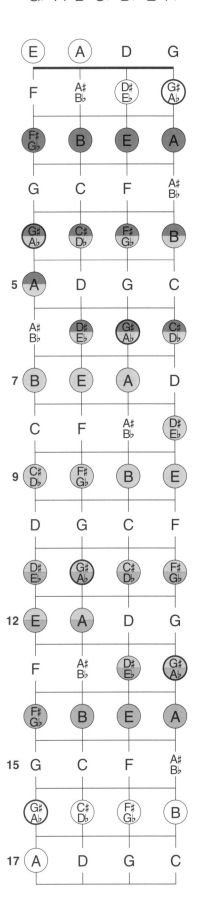

A PHRYGIAN

A–B♭–C–D–E–F–G

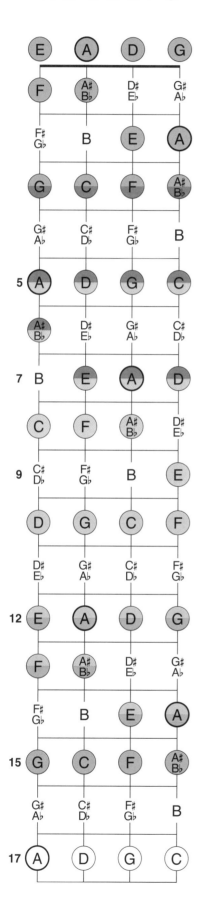

B♭ PHRYGIAN

B♭–C♭–D♭–E♭–F–G♭–A♭

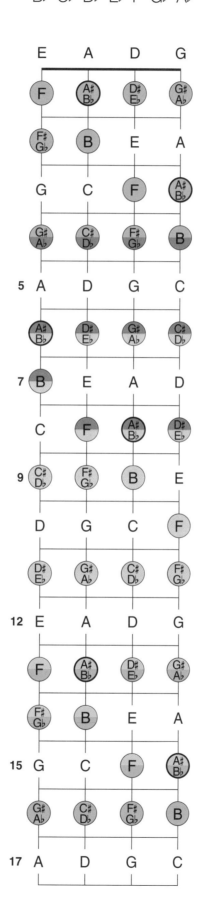

B PHRYGIAN

B–C–D–E–F♯–G–A

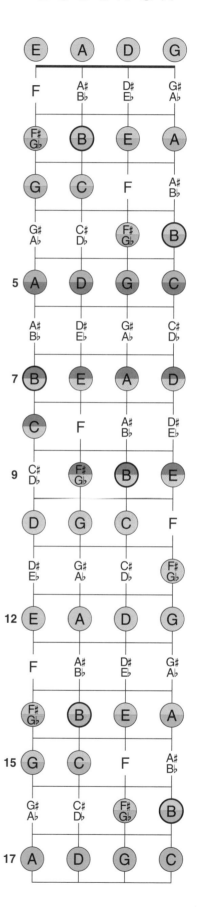

C LYDIAN

C–D–E–F#–G–A–B

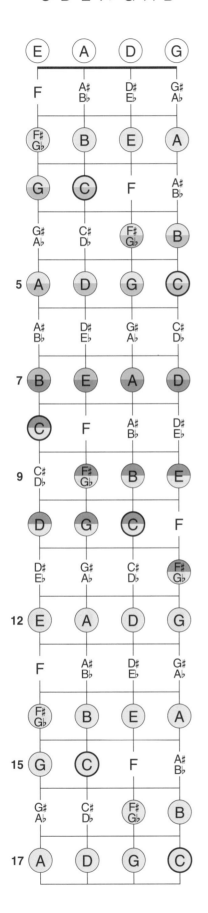

D♭ LYDIAN

D♭–E♭–F–G–A♭–B♭–C

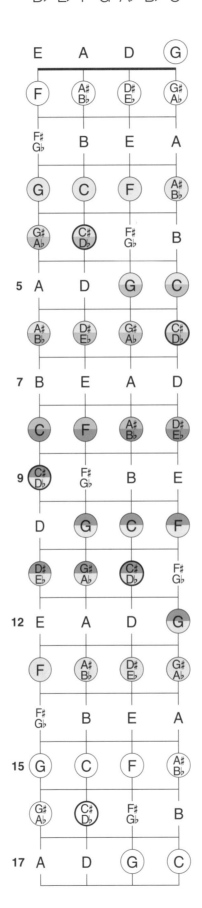

D LYDIAN

D–E–F#–G#–A–B–C#

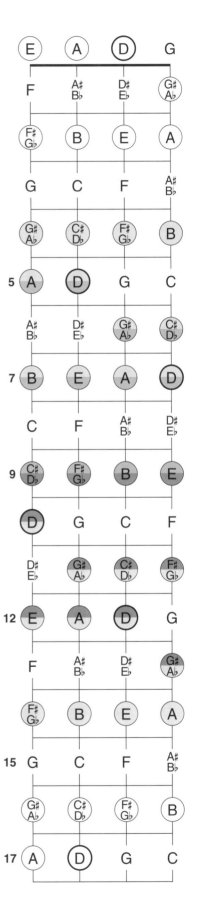

Eb LYDIAN

Eb–F–G–A–Bb–C–D

E LYDIAN

E–F#–G#–A#–B–C#–D#

F LYDIAN

F–G–A–B–C–D–E

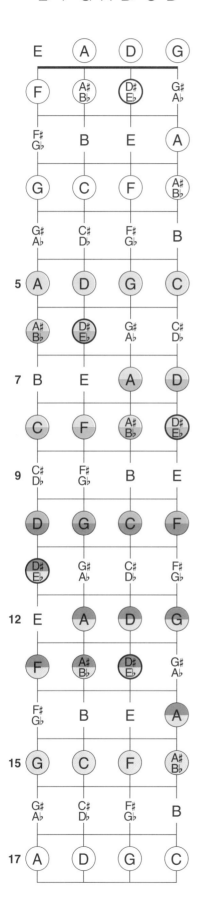

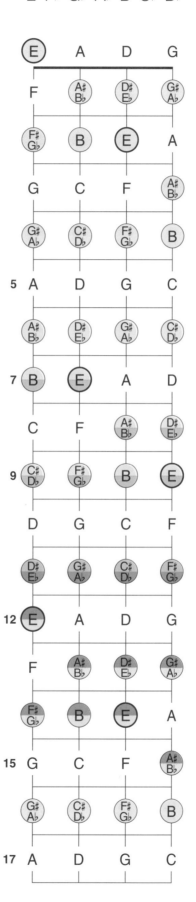

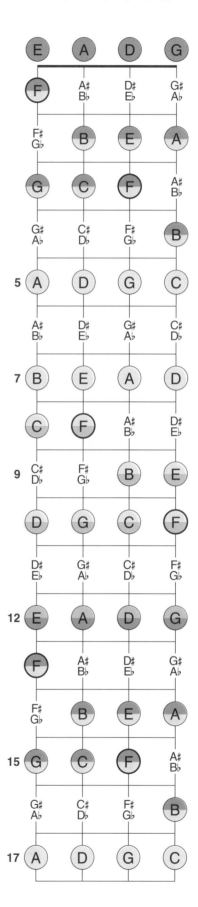

F#/G♭ LYDIAN

F#–G#–A#–B#–C#–D#–E#
G♭–A♭–B♭–C–D♭–E♭–F

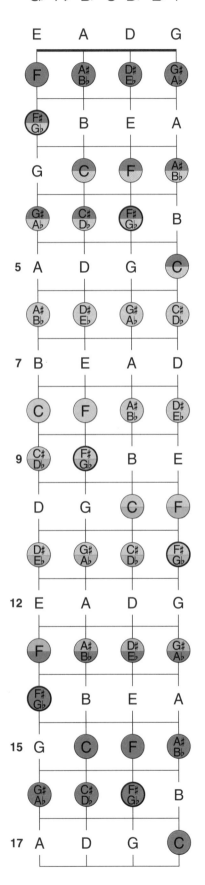

G LYDIAN

G–A–B–C#–D–E–F#

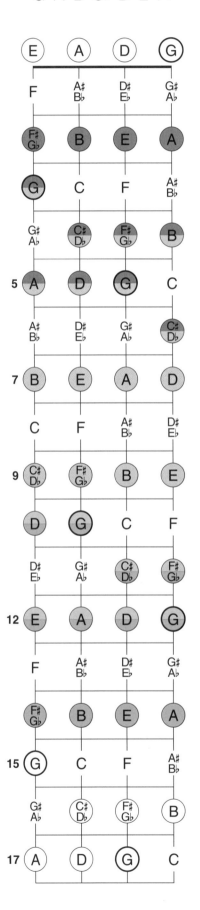

A♭ LYDIAN

A♭–B♭–C–D–E♭–F–G

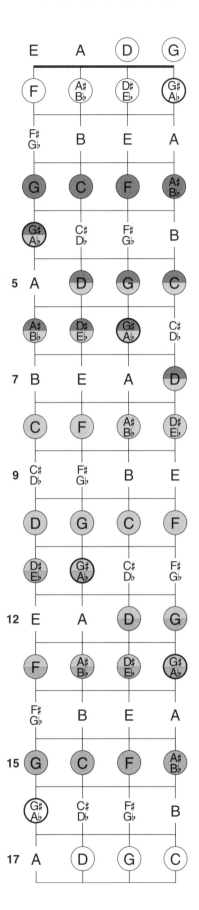

A LYDIAN

A–B–C#–D#–E–F#–G#

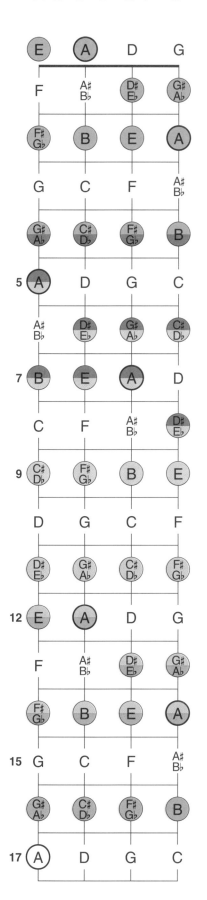

B♭ LYDIAN

B♭–C–D–E–F–G–A

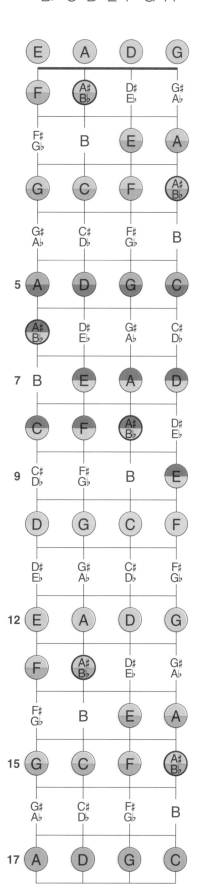

B LYDIAN

B–C#–D#–E#–F#–G#–A#

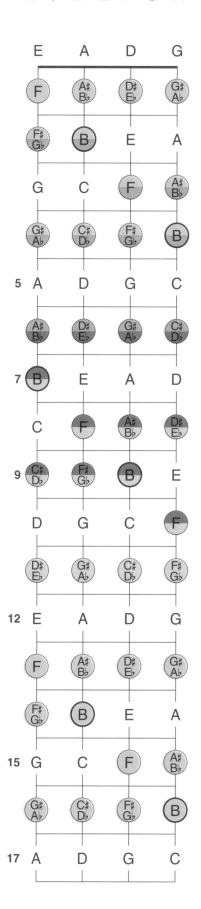

C MIXOLYDIAN

C–D–E–F–G–A–B♭

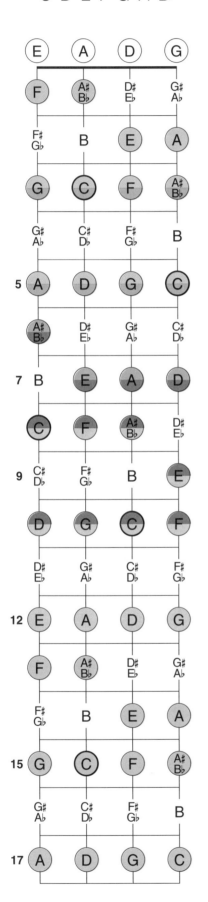

C#/D♭ MIXOLYDIAN

C#–D#–E#–F#–G#–A#–B
D♭–E♭–F–G♭–A♭–B♭–C♭

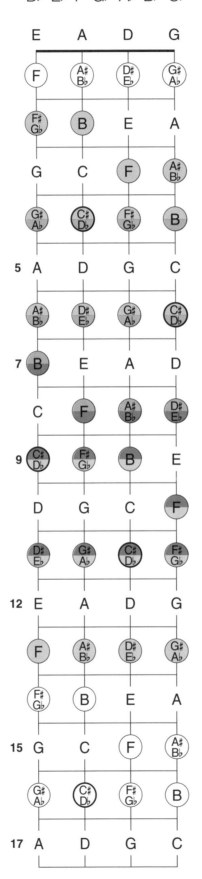

D MIXOLYDIAN

D–E–F#–G–A–B–C

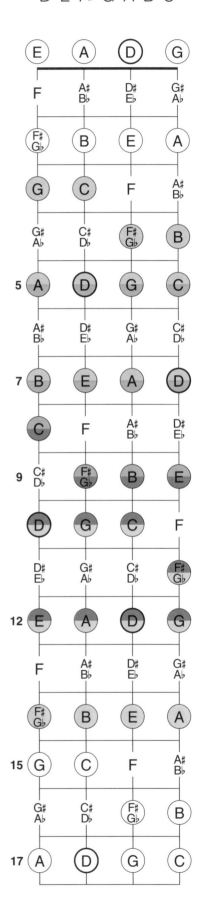

E♭ MIXOLYDIAN

E♭–F–G–A♭–B♭–C–D♭

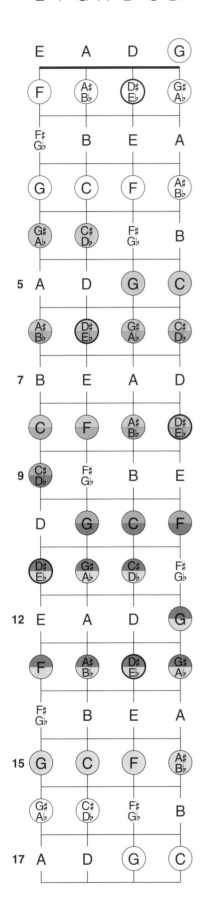

E MIXOLYDIAN

E–F#–G#–A–B–C#–D

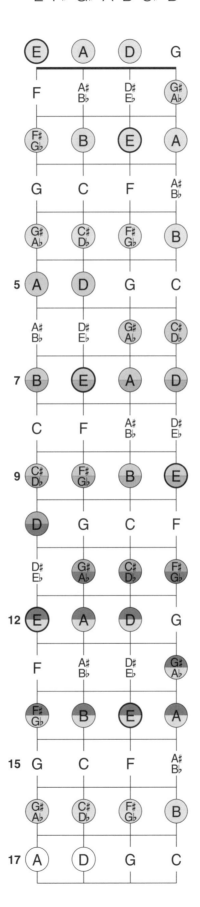

F MIXOLYDIAN

F–G–A–B♭–C–D–E♭

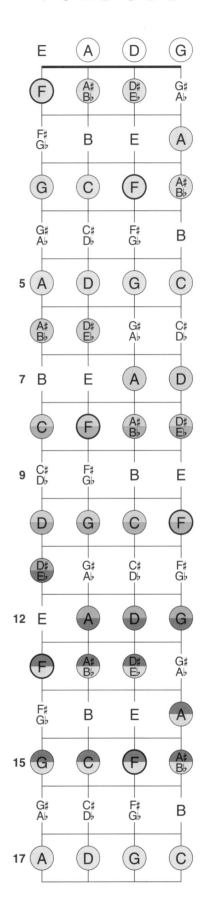

F#/G♭ MIXOLYDIAN

F#–G#–A#–B–C#–D#–E
G♭–A♭–B♭–C♭–D♭–E♭–F♭

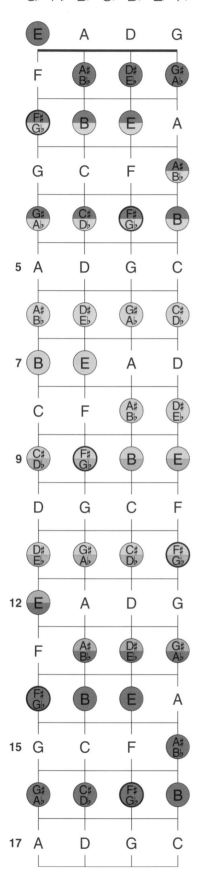

G MIXOLYDIAN

G–A–B–C–D–E–F

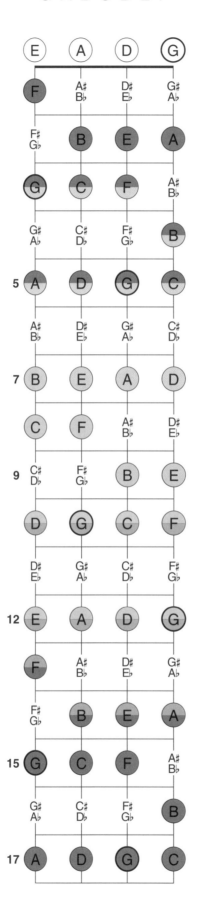

A♭ MIXOLYDIAN

A♭–B♭–C–D♭–E♭–F–G♭

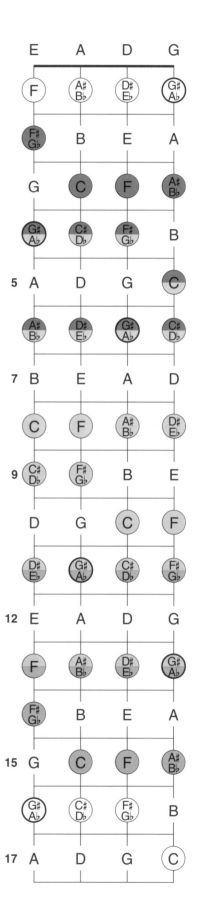

A MIXOLYDIAN

A–B–C#–D–E–F#–G

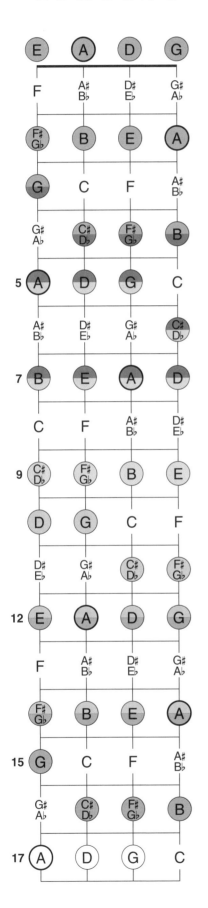

B♭ MIXOLYDIAN

B♭–C–D–E♭–F–G–A♭

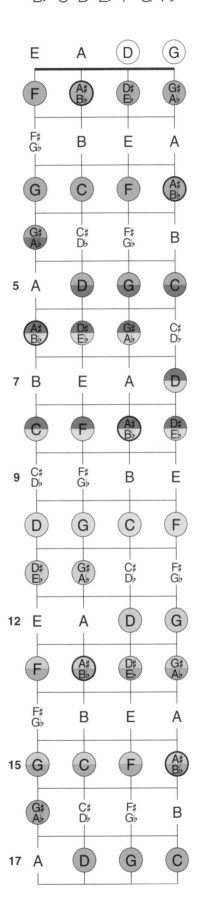

B MIXOLYDIAN

B–C#–D#–E–F#–G#–A

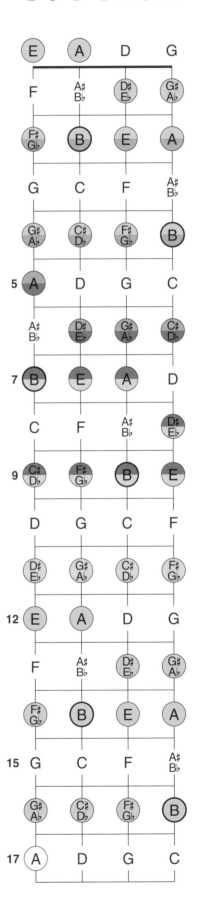

27

C AEOLIAN

C–D–E♭–F–G–A♭–B♭

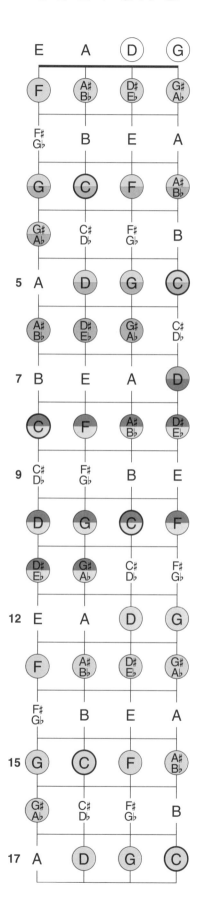

C♯ AEOLIAN

C♯–D♯–E–F♯–G♯–A–B

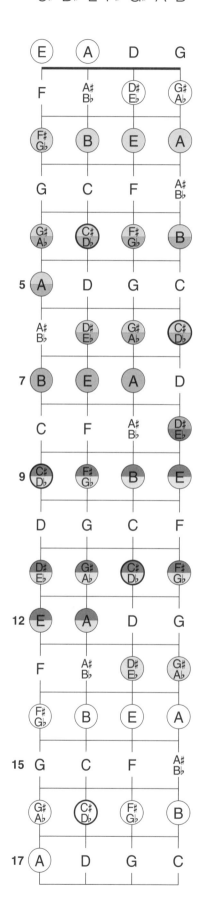

D AEOLIAN

D–E–F–G–A–B♭–C

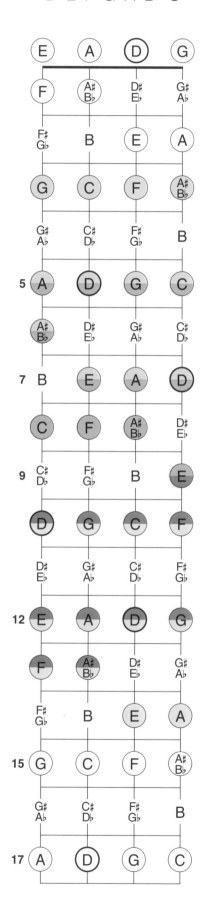

D♯/E♭ AEOLIAN

D♯–E♯–F♯–G♯–A♯–B–C♯
E♭–F–G♭–A♭–B♭–C♭–D♭

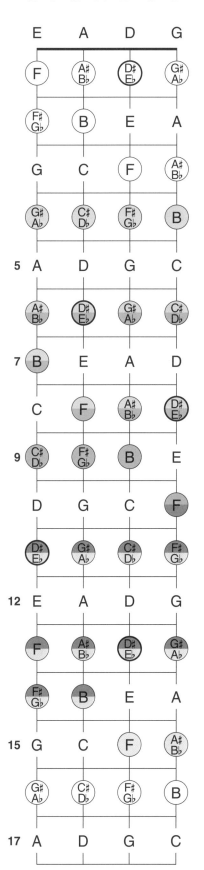

E AEOLIAN

E–F♯–G–A–B–C–D

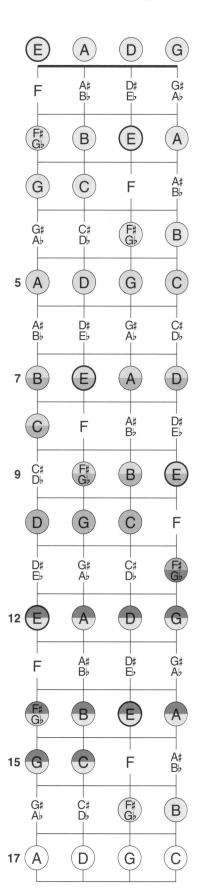

F AEOLIAN

F–G–A♭–B♭–C–D♭–E♭

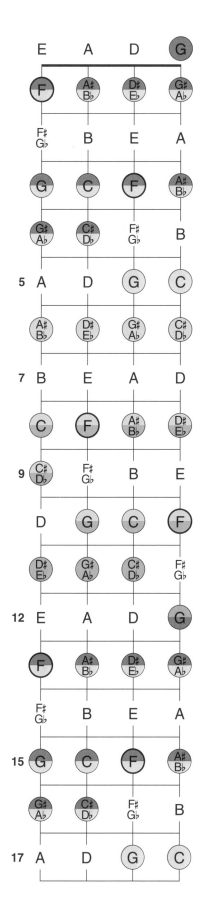

F♯ AEOLIAN

F♯–G♯–A–B–C♯–D–E

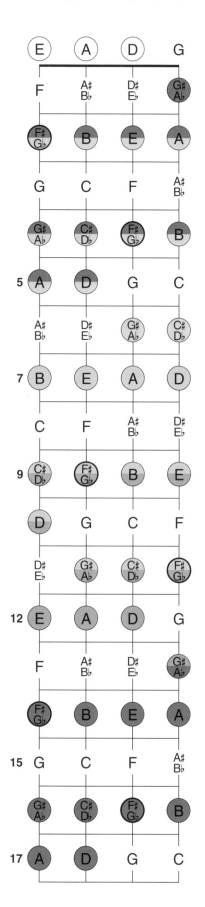

G AEOLIAN

G–A–B♭–C–D–E♭–F

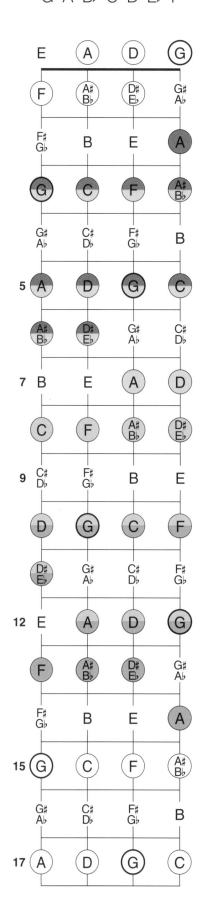

A♭ AEOLIAN

A♭–B♭–C♭–D♭–E♭–F♭–G♭

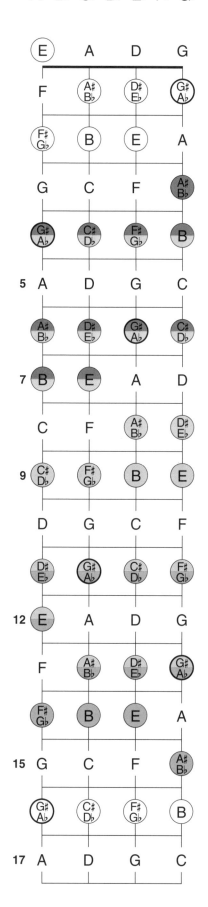

A AEOLIAN

A–B–C–D–E–F–G

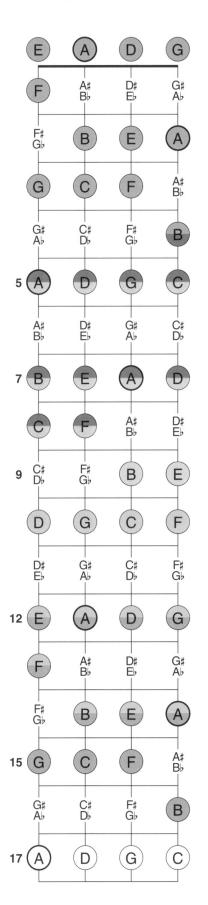

B♭ AEOLIAN

B♭–C–D♭–E♭–F–G♭–A♭

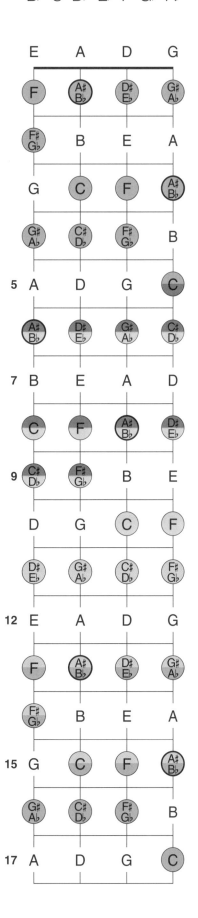

B AEOLIAN

B–C#–D–E–F#–G–A

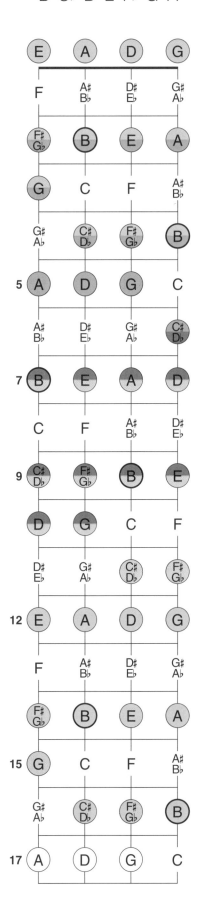

C LOCRIAN

C–Db–Eb–F–Gb–Ab–Bb

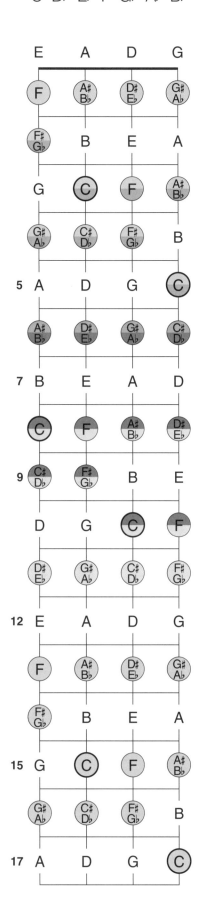

C# LOCRIAN

C#–D–E–F#–G–A–B

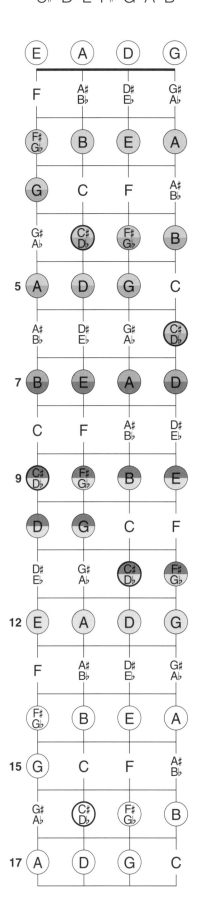

D LOCRIAN

D–Eb–F–G–Ab–Bb–C

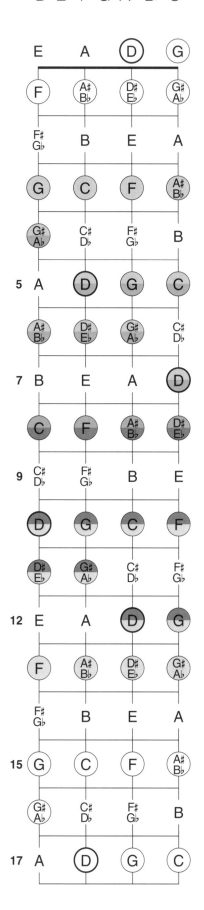

D♯ LOCRIAN

D♯–E–F♯–G♯–A–B–C♯

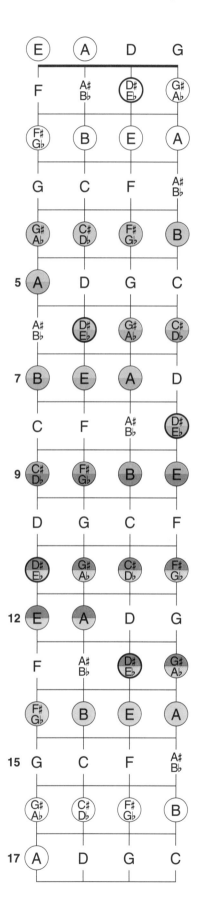

E LOCRIAN

E–F–G–A–B♭–C–D

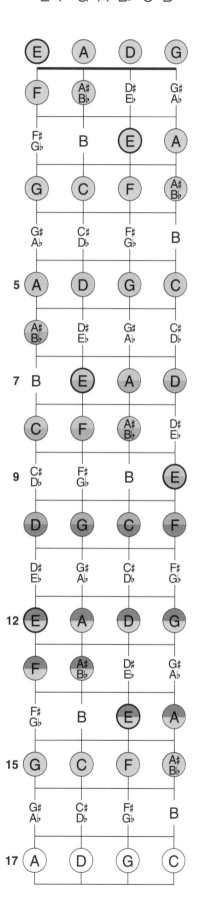

F LOCRIAN

F–G♭–A♭–B♭–C♭–D♭–E♭

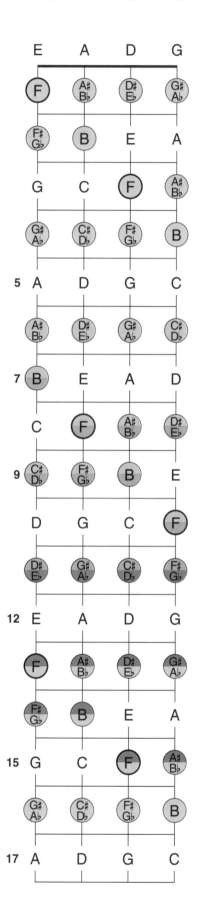

F# LOCRIAN

F#–G–A–B–C–D–E

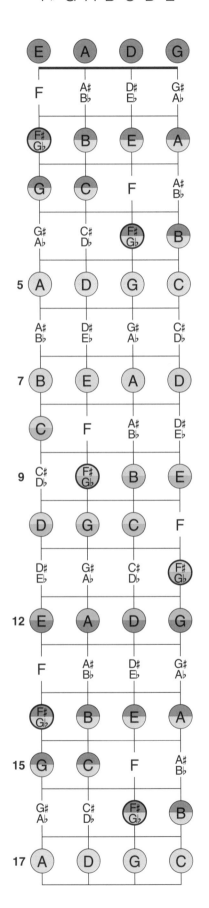

G LOCRIAN

G–A♭–B♭–C–D♭–E♭–F

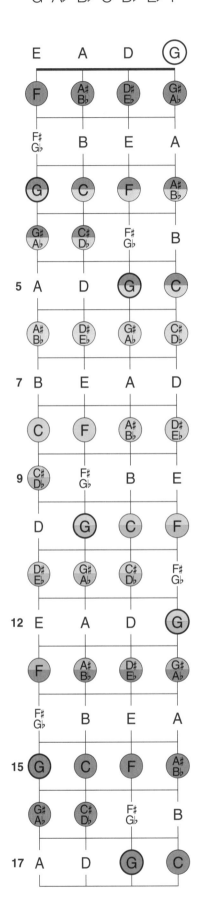

G# LOCRIAN

G#–A–B–C#–D–E–F#

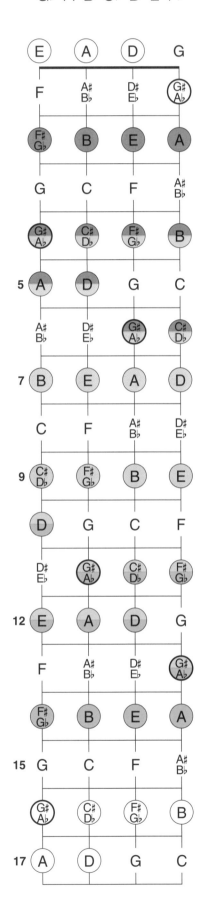

A LOCRIAN

A–B♭–C–D–E♭–F–G

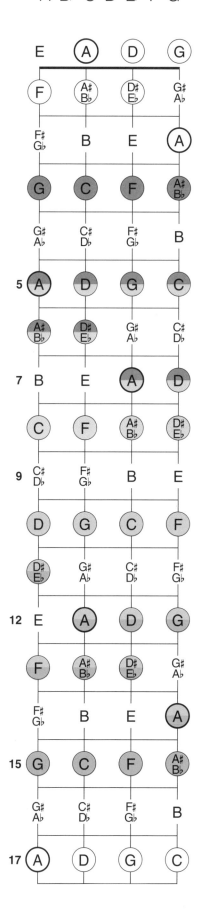

A♯ LOCRIAN

A♯–B–C♯–D♯–E–F♯–G♯

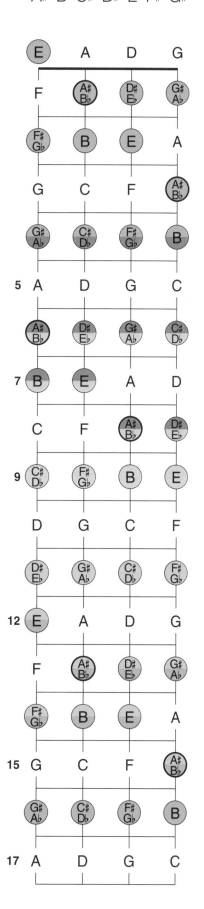

B LOCRIAN

B–C–D–E–F–G–A

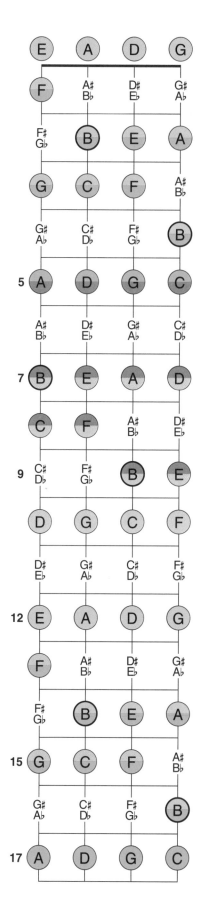

35

SCALES

PENTATONIC AND BLUES SCALES

C MAJOR PENTATONIC

C–D–E–G–A

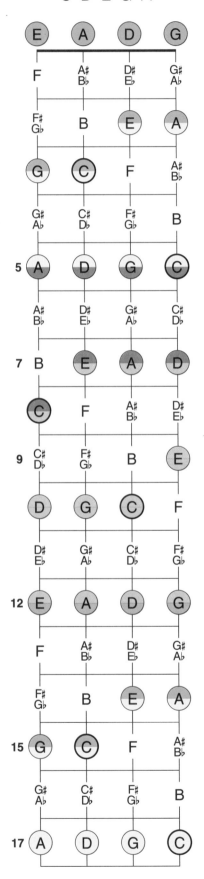

D♭ MAJOR PENTATONIC

D♭–E♭–F–A♭–B♭

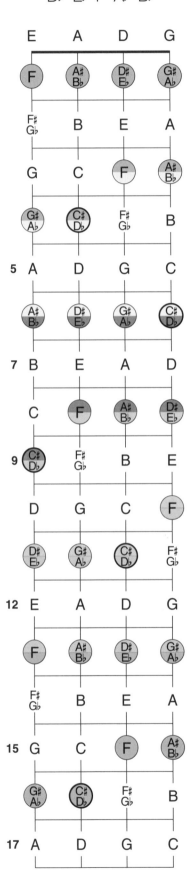

D MAJOR PENTATONIC

D–E–F♯–A–B

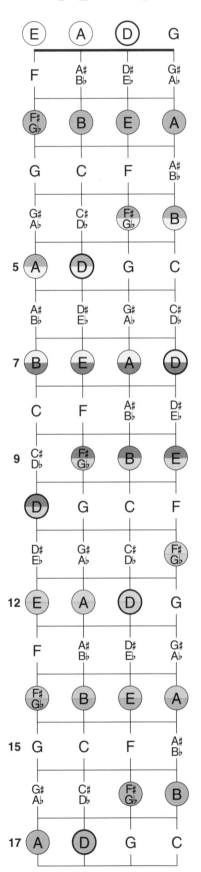

E♭ MAJOR PENTATONIC

E♭–F–G–B♭–C

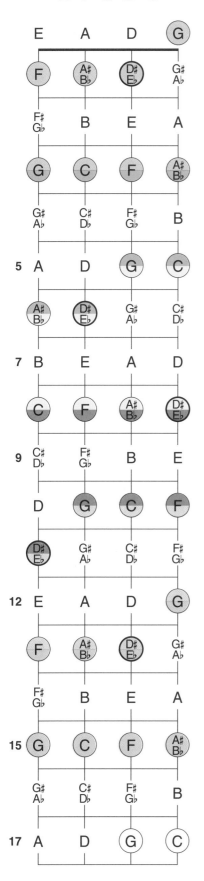

E MAJOR PENTATONIC

E–F#–G#–B–C#

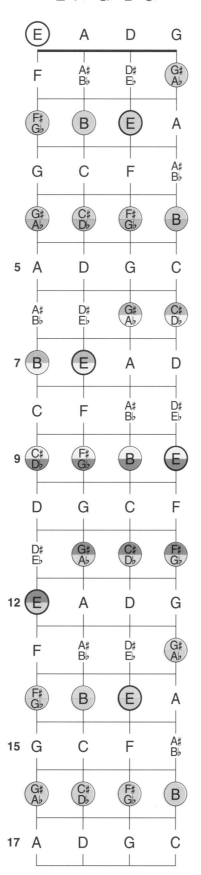

F MAJOR PENTATONIC

F–G–A–C–D

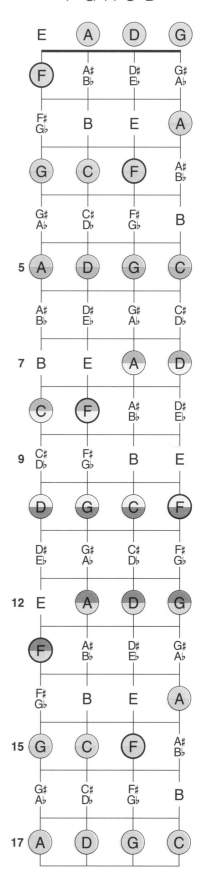

G♭ MAJOR PENTATONIC

G♭–A♭–B♭–D♭–E♭

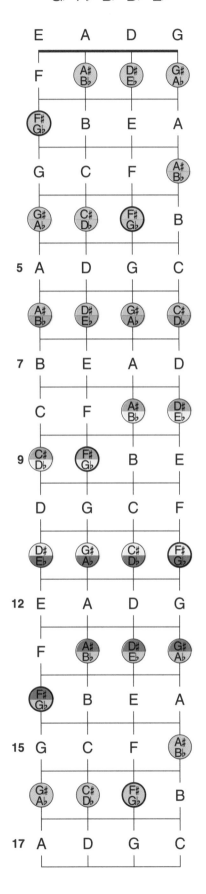

G MAJOR PENTATONIC

G–A–B–D–E

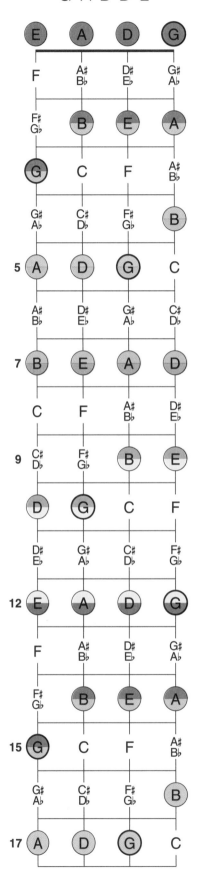

A♭ MAJOR PENTATONIC

A♭–B♭–C–E♭–F

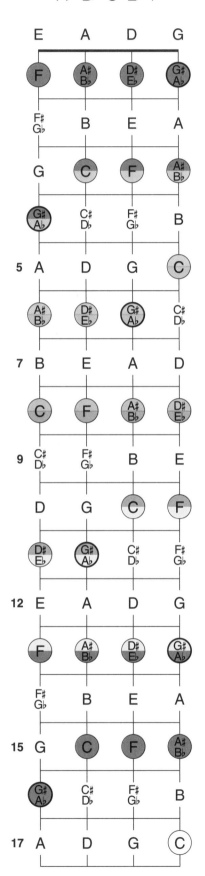

A MAJOR PENTATONIC

A–B–C#–E–F#

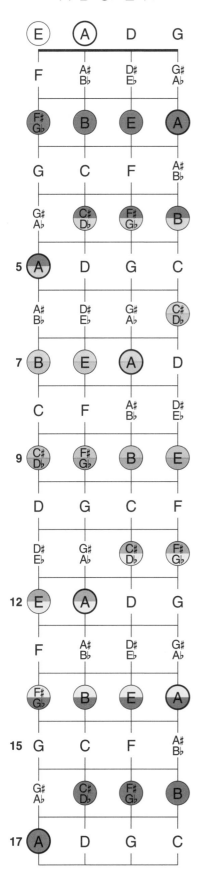

Bb MAJOR PENTATONIC

Bb–C–D–F–G

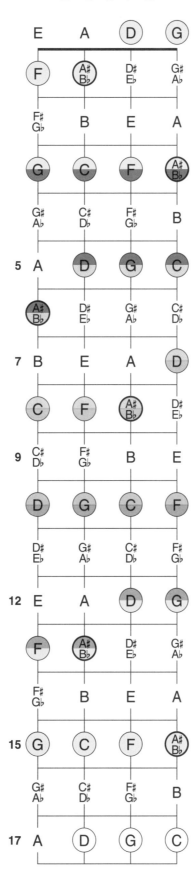

B MAJOR PENTATONIC

B–C#–D#–F#–G#

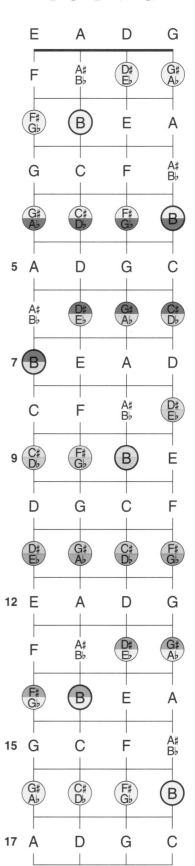

C MINOR PENTATONIC

C–E♭–F–G–B♭

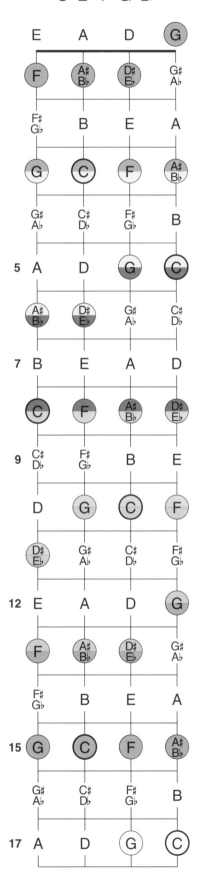

C♯ MINOR PENTATONIC

C♯–E–F♯–G♯–B

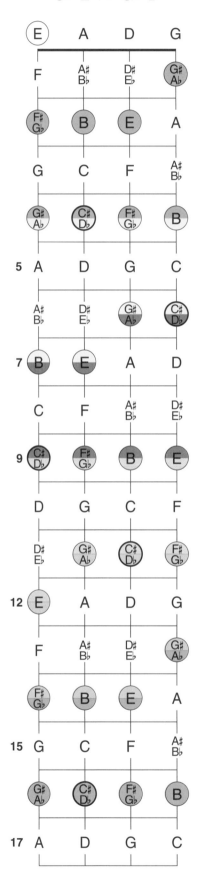

D MINOR PENTATONIC

D–F–G–A–C

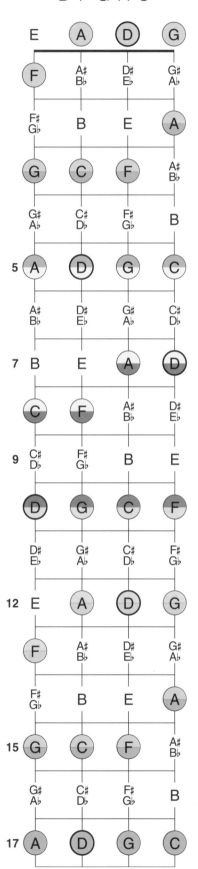

Eb MINOR PENTATONIC

Eb–Gb–Ab–Bb–Db

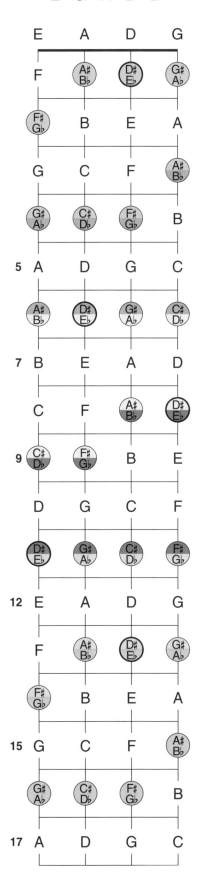

E MINOR PENTATONIC

E–G–A–B–D

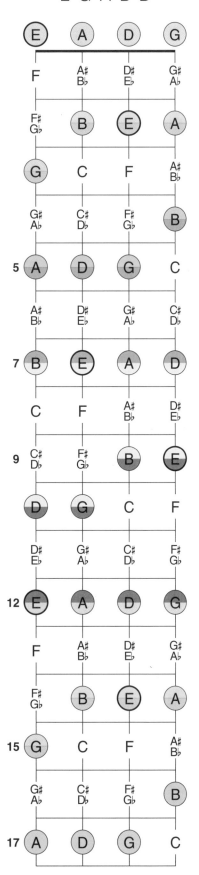

F MINOR PENTATONIC

F–Ab–Bb–C–Eb

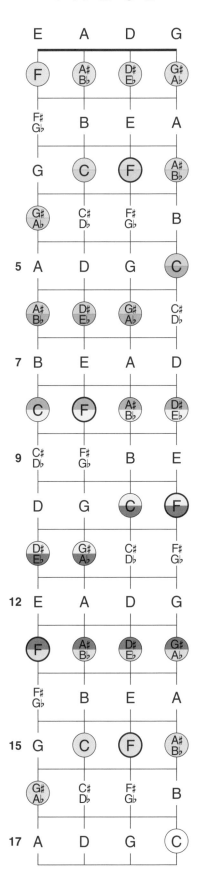

F# MINOR PENTATONIC

F#–A–B–C#–E

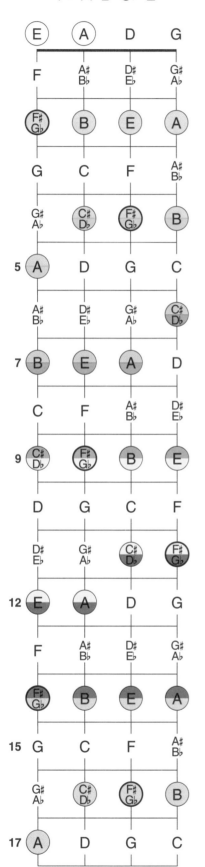

G MINOR PENTATONIC

G–Bb–C–D–F

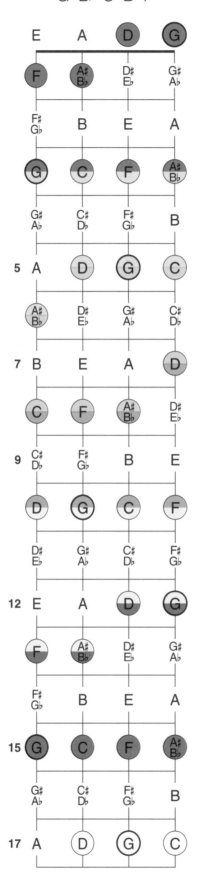

Ab MINOR PENTATONIC

Ab–Cb–Db–Eb–Gb

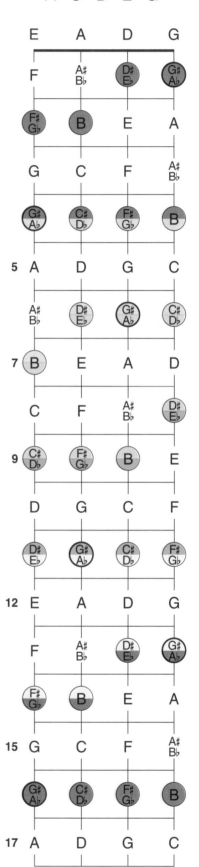

A MINOR PENTATONIC
A–C–D–E–G

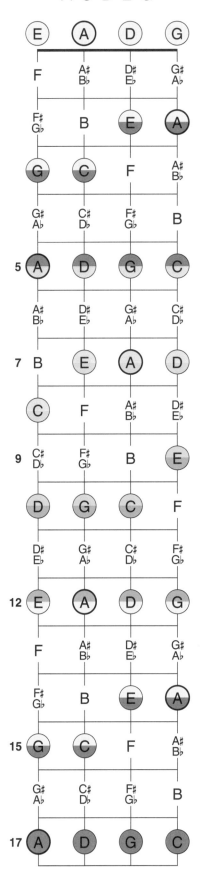

Bb MINOR PENTATONIC
Bb–Db–Eb–F–Ab

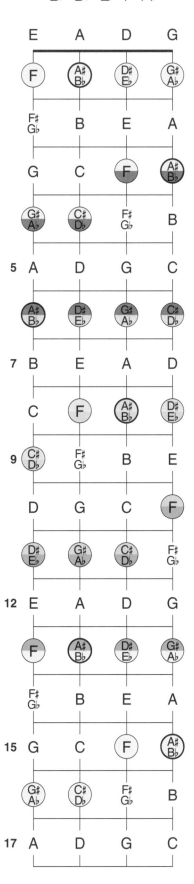

B MINOR PENTATONIC
B–D–E–F#–A

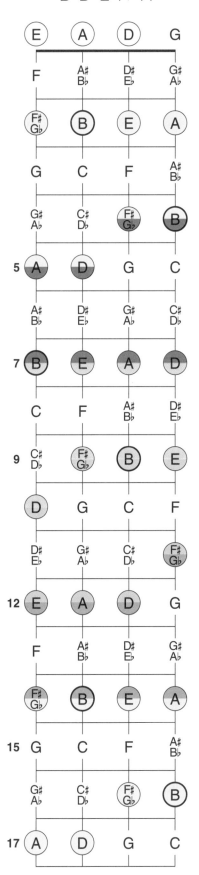

C BLUES

C–E♭–F–G♭–G–B♭

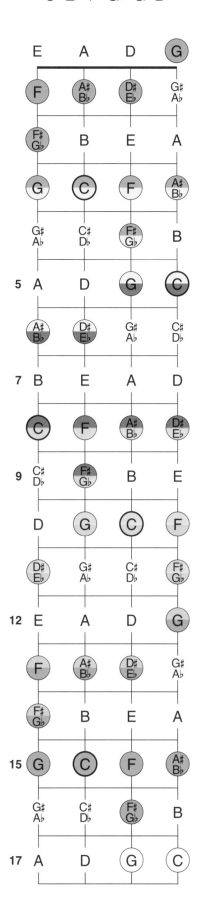

C# BLUES

C#–E–F#–G–G#–B

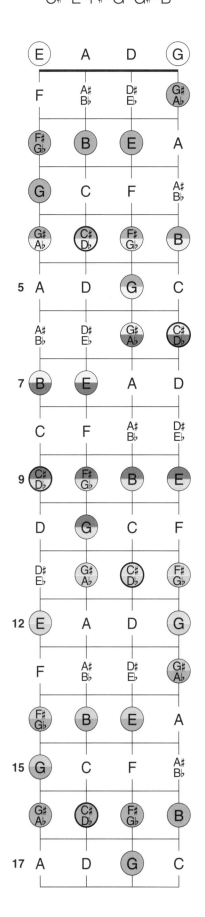

D BLUES

D–F–G–A♭–A–C

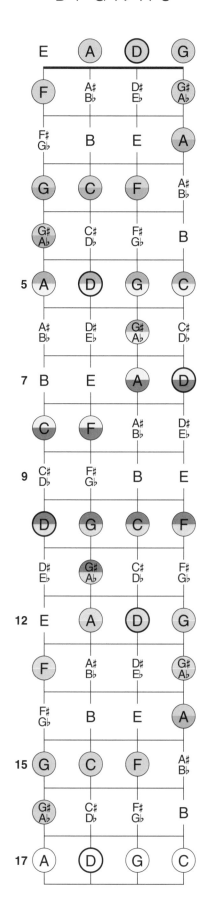

Eb BLUES

Eb–Gb–Ab–A–Bb–Db

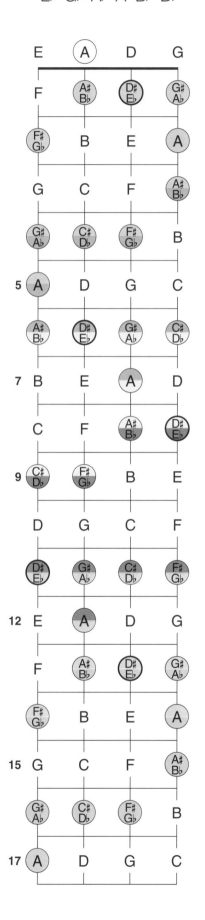

E BLUES

E–G–A–Bb–B–D

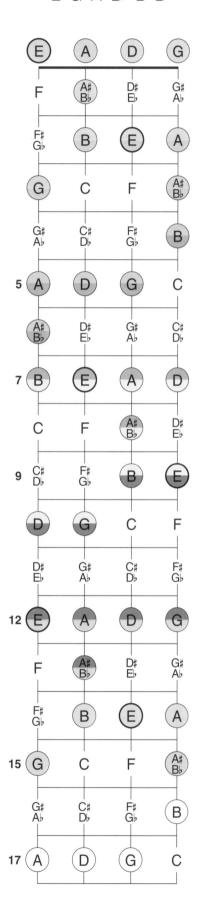

F BLUES

F–Ab–Bb–Cb–C–Eb

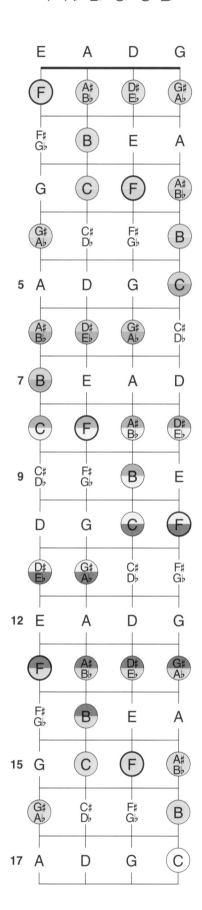

F♯ BLUES

F♯–A–B–C–C♯–E

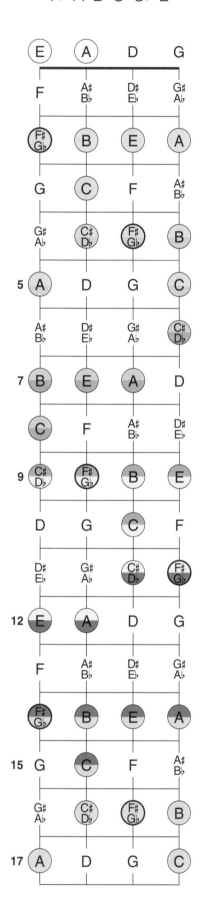

G BLUES

G–B♭–C–D♭–D–F

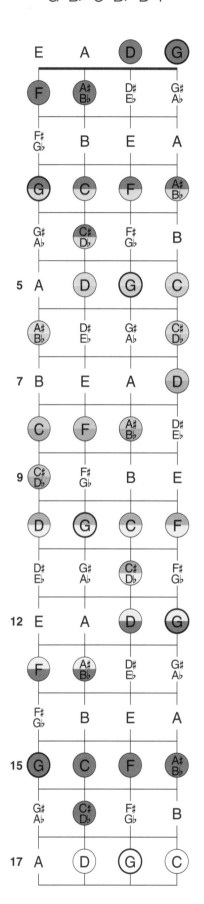

A♭ BLUES

A♭–C♭–D♭–D–E♭–G♭

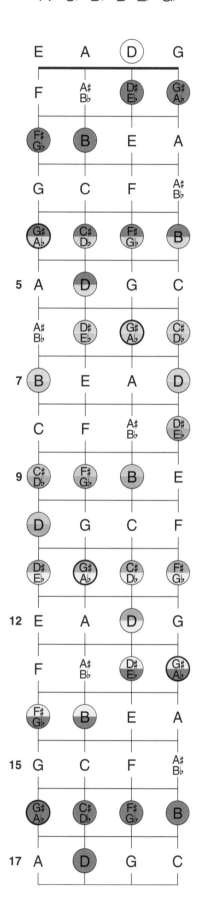

A BLUES

A–C–D–E♭–E–G

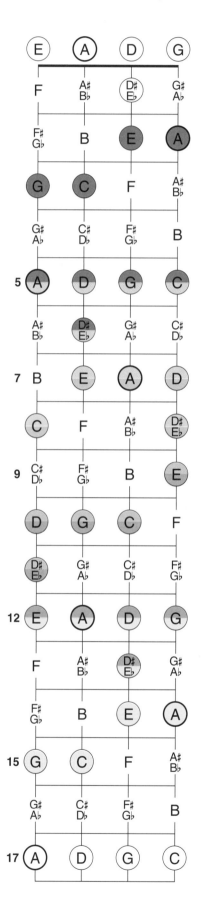

B♭ BLUES

B♭–D♭–E♭–E–F–A♭

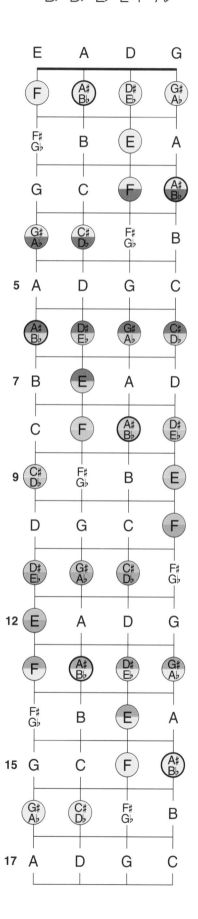

B BLUES

B–D–E–F–F♯–A

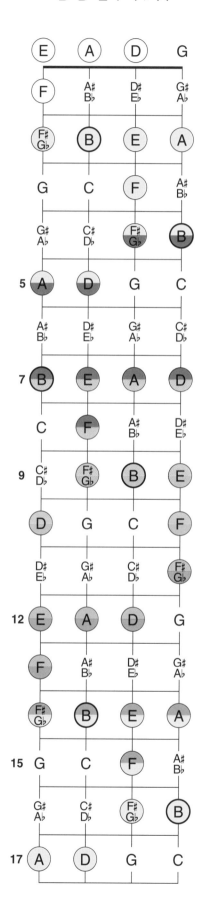

SCALES

THE MELODIC MINOR SCALE AND ITS MODES

C MELODIC MINOR

C–D–E♭–F–G–A–B

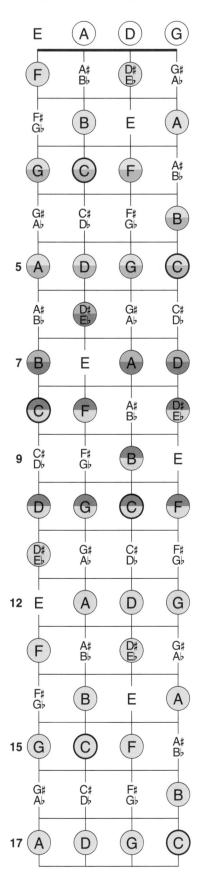

C# MELODIC MINOR

C♯–D♯–E–F♯–G♯–A♯–B♯

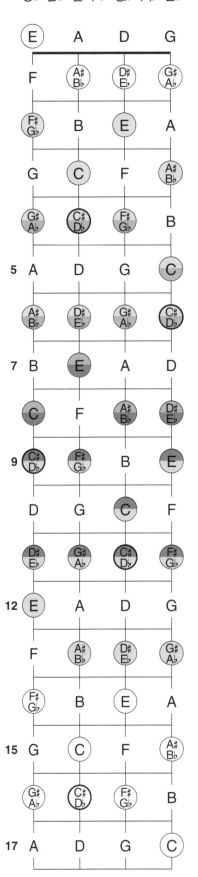

D MELODIC MINOR

D–E–F–G–A–B–C♯

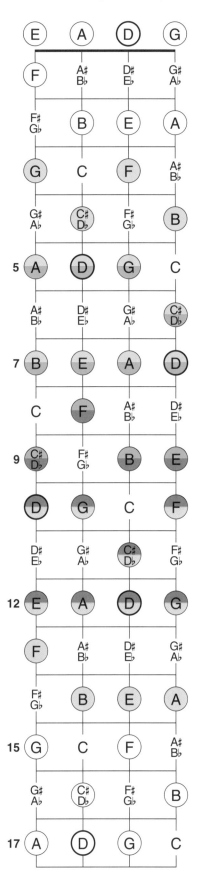

E♭ MELODIC MINOR

E♭–F–G♭–A♭–B♭–C–D

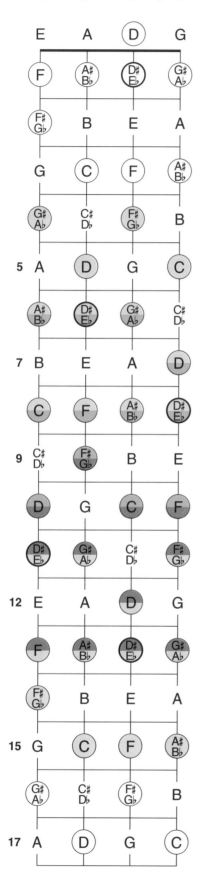

E MELODIC MINOR

E–F#–G–A–B–C#–D#

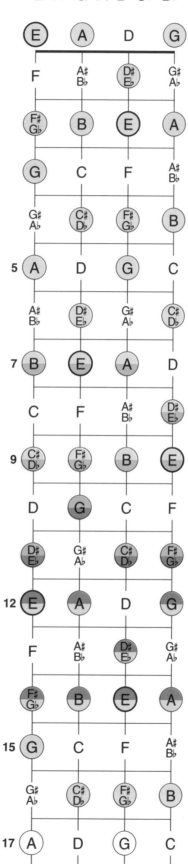

F MELODIC MINOR

F–G–A♭–B♭–C–D–E

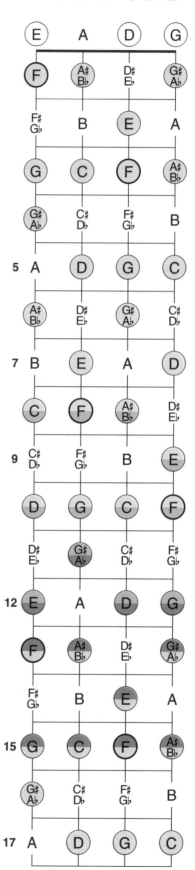

F♯ MELODIC MINOR

F♯–G♯–A–B–C♯–D♯–E♯

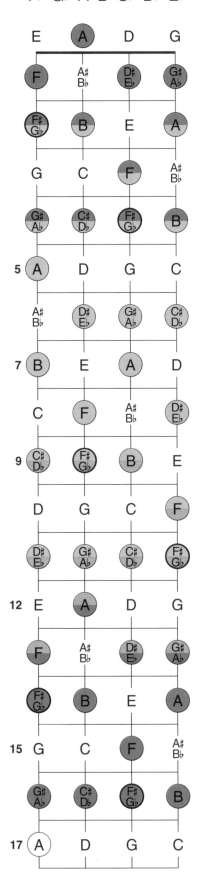

G MELODIC MINOR

G–A–B♭–C–D–E–F♯

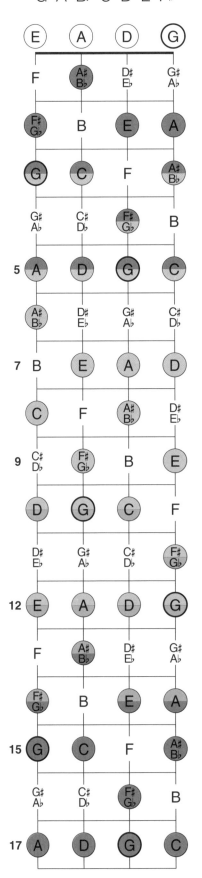

A♭ MELODIC MINOR

A♭–B♭–C♭–D♭–E♭–F–G

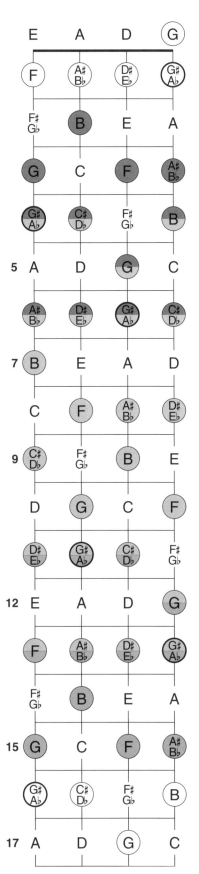

A MELODIC MINOR

A–B–C–D–E–F#–G#

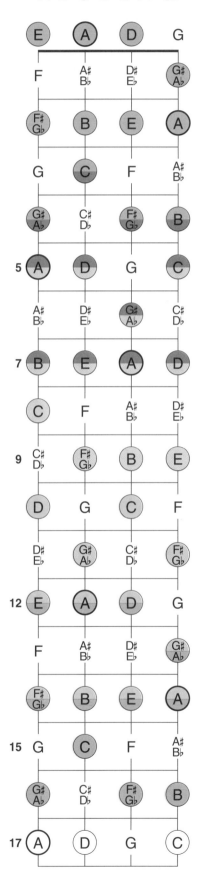

Bb MELODIC MINOR

Bb–C–Db–Eb–F–G–A

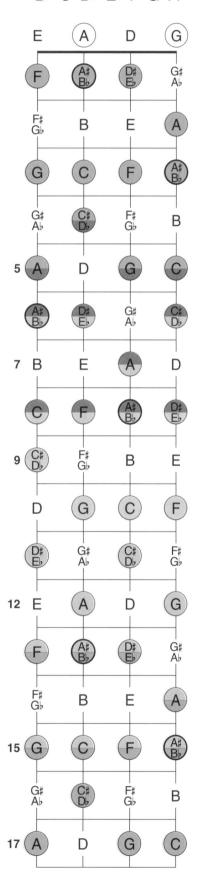

B MELODIC MINOR

B–C#–D–E–F#–G#–A#

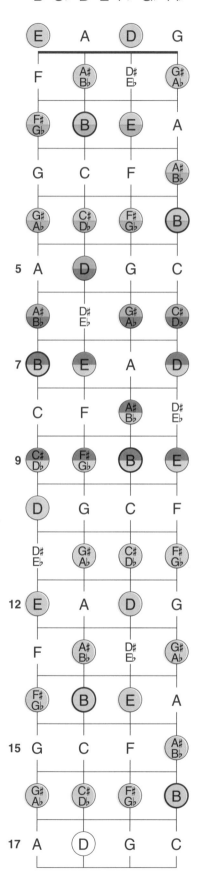

55

C DORIAN ♭2

C–D♭–E♭–F–G–A–B♭

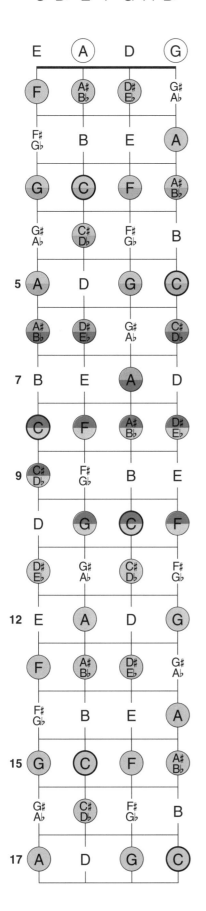

C# DORIAN ♭2

C#–D–E–F#–G#–A#–B

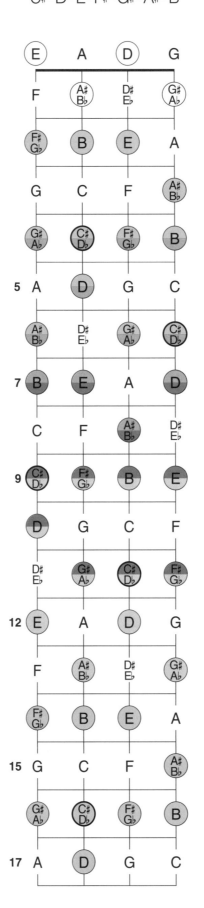

D DORIAN ♭2

D–E♭–F–G–A–B–C

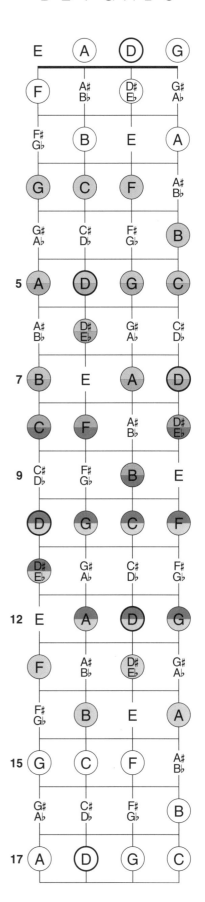

E♭ DORIAN ♭2

E♭–F♭–G♭–A♭–B♭–C–D♭

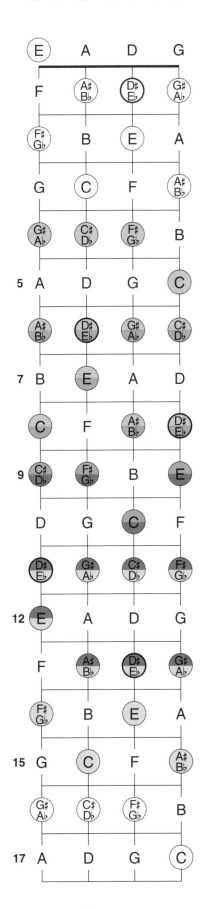

E DORIAN ♭2

E–F–G–A–B–C#–D

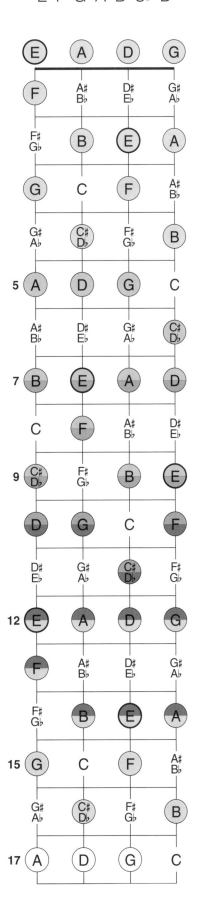

F DORIAN ♭2

F–G♭–A♭–B♭–C–D–E♭

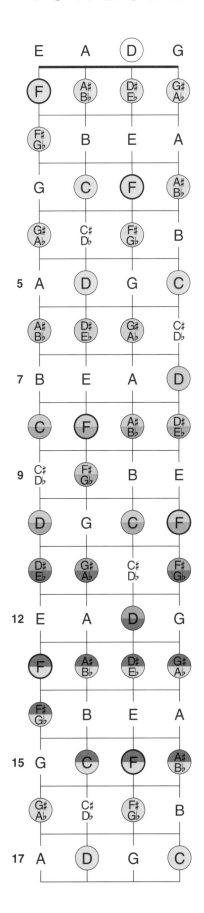

F# DORIAN ♭2

F#–G–A–B–C#–D#–E

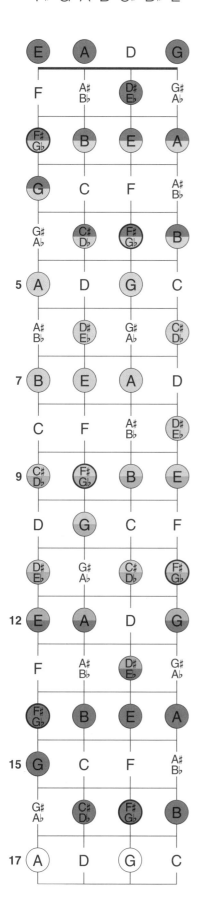

G DORIAN ♭2

G–A♭–B♭–C–D–E–F

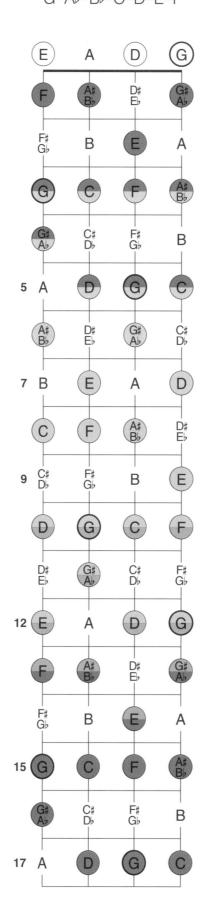

G# DORIAN ♭2

G#–A–B–C#–D#–E#–F#

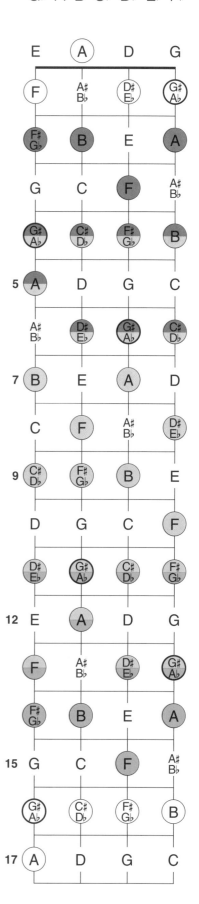

A DORIAN ♭2

A–B♭–C–D–E–F#–G

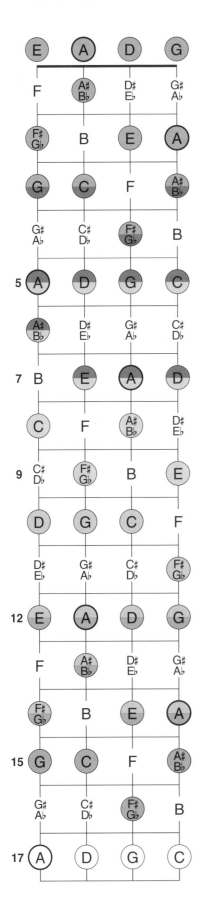

B♭ DORIAN ♭2

B♭–C♭–D♭–E♭–F–G–A♭

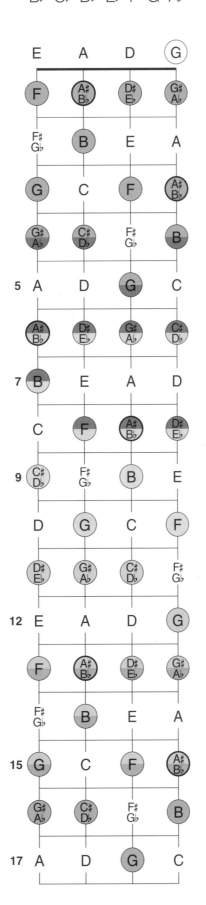

B DORIAN ♭2

B–C–D–E–F#–G#–A

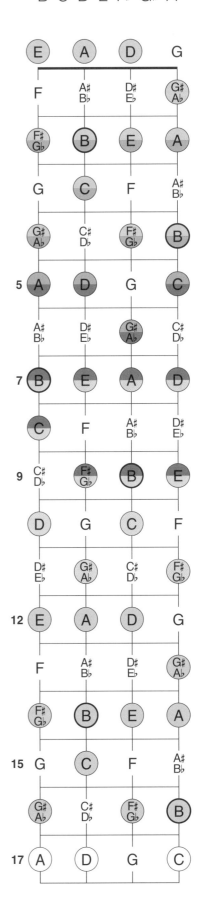

C LYDIAN AUGMENTED

C–D–E–F#–G#–A–B

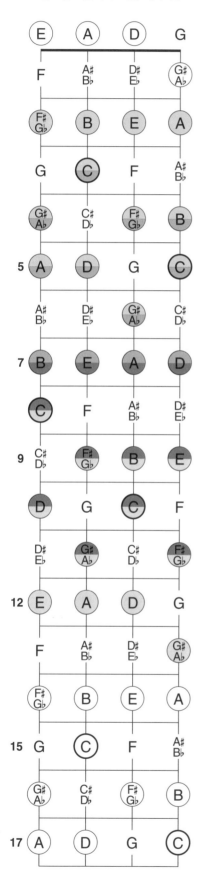

Db LYDIAN AUGMENTED

Db–Eb–F–G–A–Bb–C

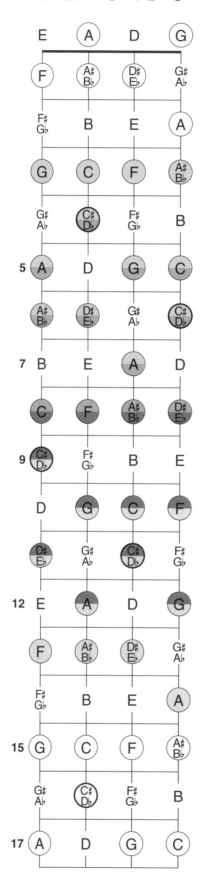

D LYDIAN AUGMENTED

D–E–F#–G#–A#–B–C#

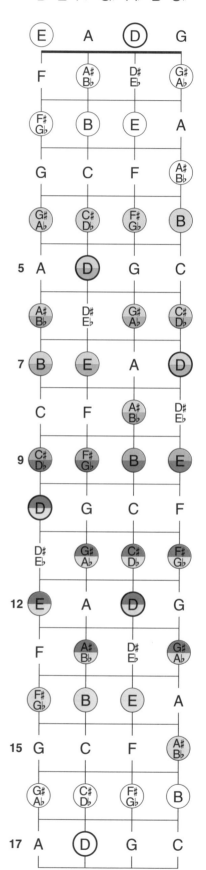

Eb LYDIAN AUGMENTED

Eb–F–G–A–B–C–D

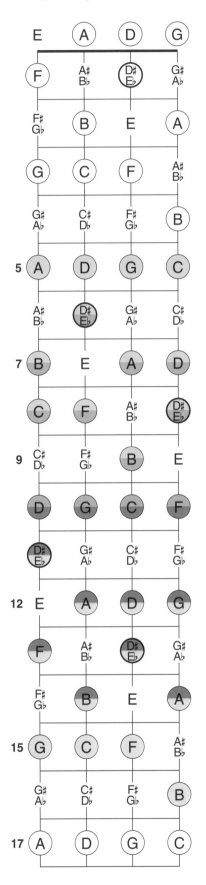

E LYDIAN AUGMENTED

E–F#–G#–A#–B#–C#–D#

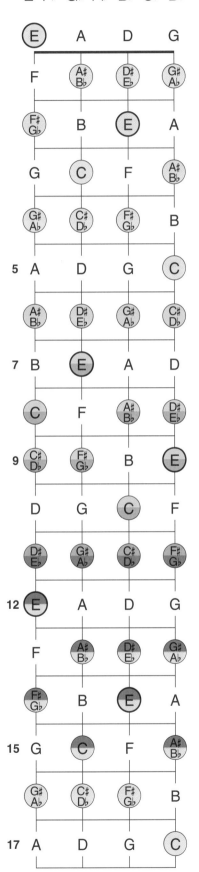

F LYDIAN AUGMENTED

F–G–A–B–C#–D–E

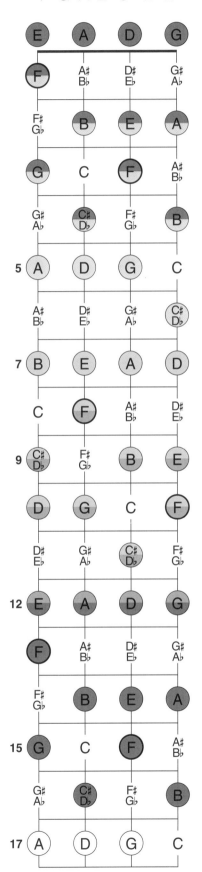

G♭ LYDIAN AUGMENTED

G♭–A♭–B♭–C–D–E♭–F

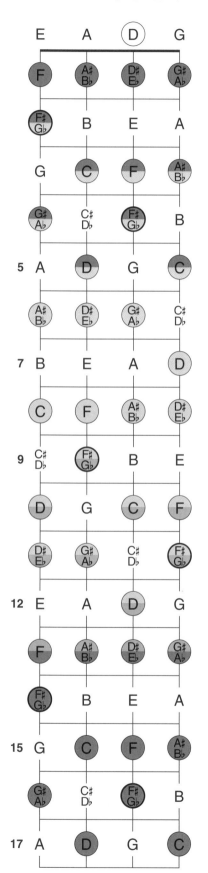

G LYDIAN AUGMENTED

G–A–B–C♯–D♯–E–F♯

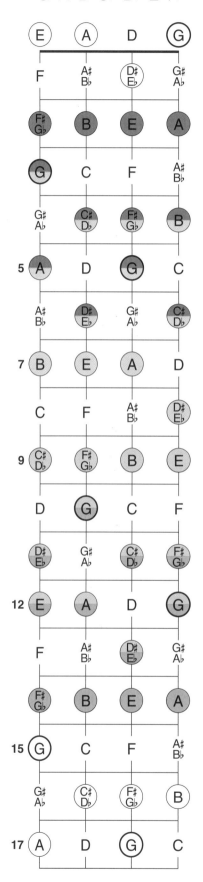

A♭ LYDIAN AUGMENTED

A♭–B♭–C–D–E–F–G

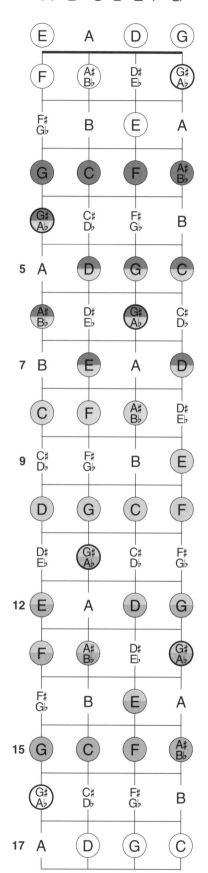

A LYDIAN AUGMENTED

A–B–C#–D#–E#–F#–G#

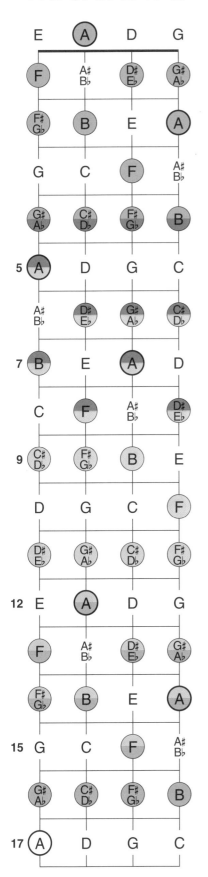

B♭ LYDIAN AUGMENTED

B♭–C–D–E–F#–G–A

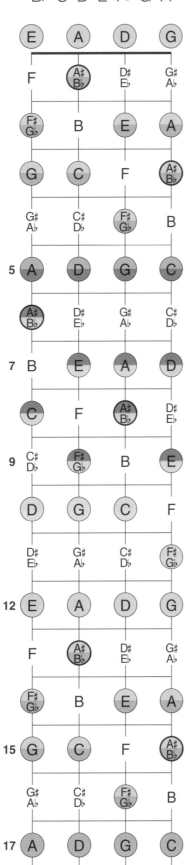

B LYDIAN AUGMENTED

B–C#–D#–E#–F×–G#–A#

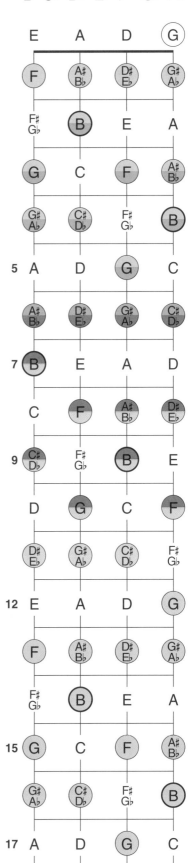

63

C LYDIAN DOMINANT

C–D–E–F#–G–A–Bb

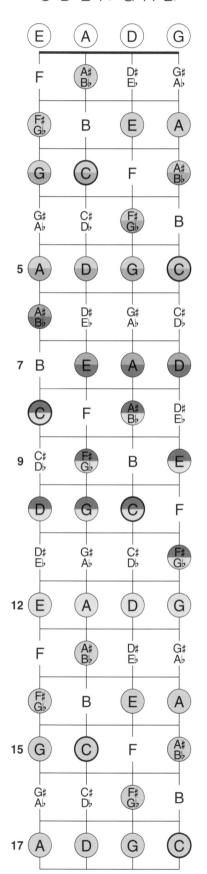

Db LYDIAN DOMINANT

Db–Eb–F–G–Ab–Bb–Cb

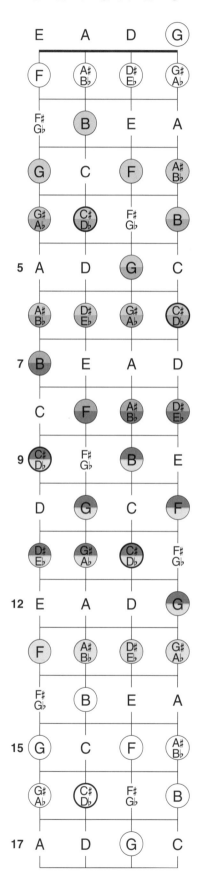

D LYDIAN DOMINANT

D–E–F#–G#–A–B–C

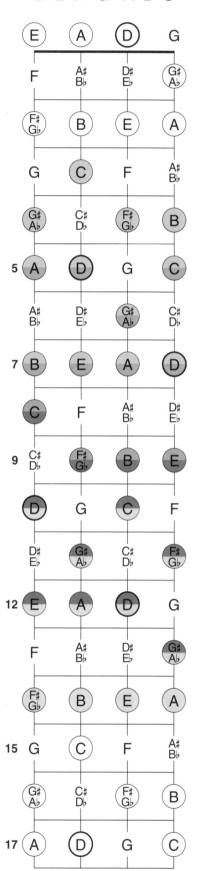

Eb LYDIAN DOMINANT

Eb–F–G–A–Bb–C–Db

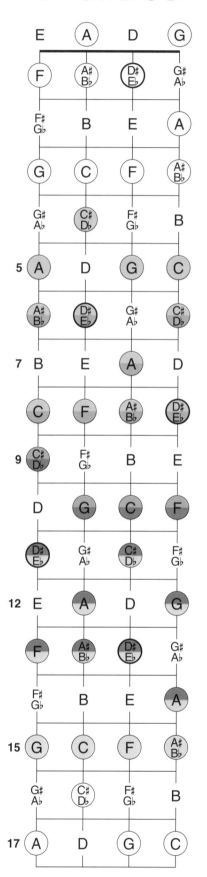

E LYDIAN DOMINANT

E–F#–G#–A#–B–C#–D

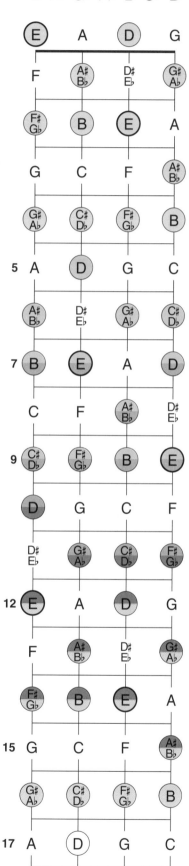

F LYDIAN DOMINANT

F–G–A–B–C–D–Eb

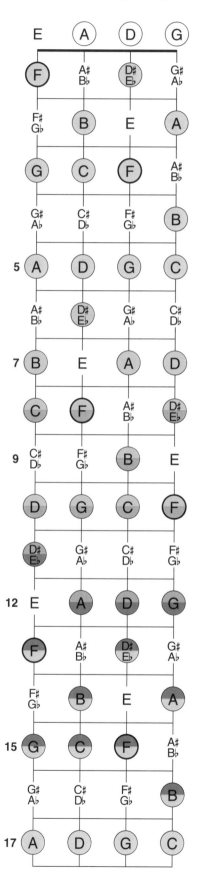

G♭ LYDIAN DOMINANT

G♭–A♭–B♭–C–D♭–E♭–F♭

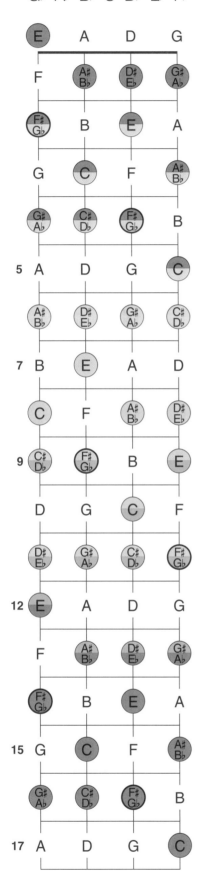

G LYDIAN DOMINANT

G–A–B–C#–D–E–F

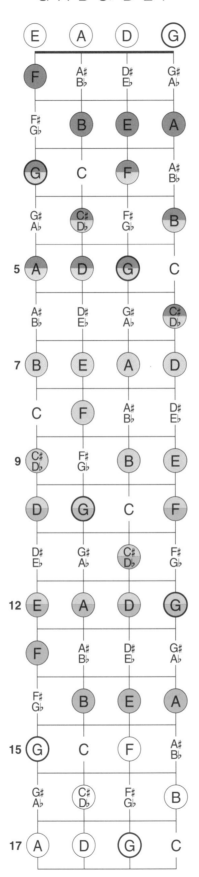

A♭ LYDIAN DOMINANT

A♭–B♭–C–D–E♭–F–G♭

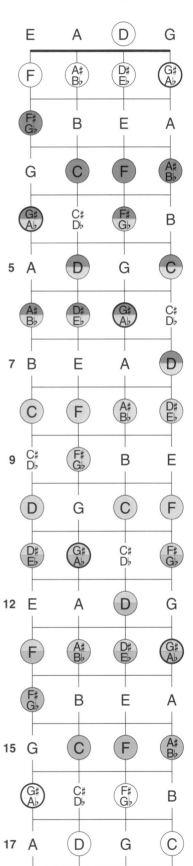

A LYDIAN DOMINANT

A–B–C#–D#–E–F#–G

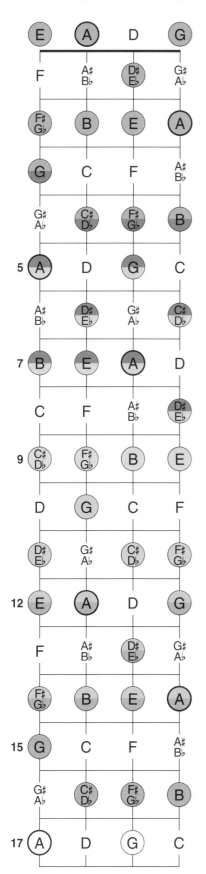

B♭ LYDIAN DOMINANT

B♭–C–D–E–F–G–A♭

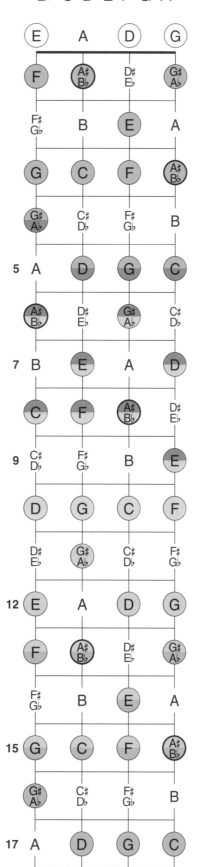

B LYDIAN DOMINANT

B–C#–D#–E#–F#–G#–A

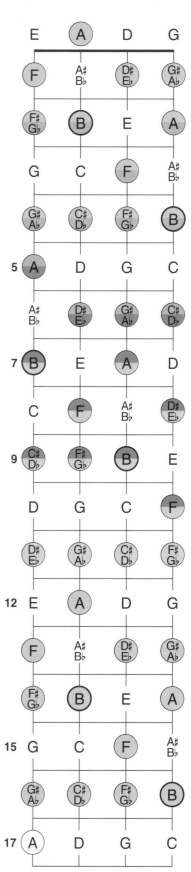

67

C MIXOLYDIAN ♭6

C–D–E–F–G–A♭–B♭

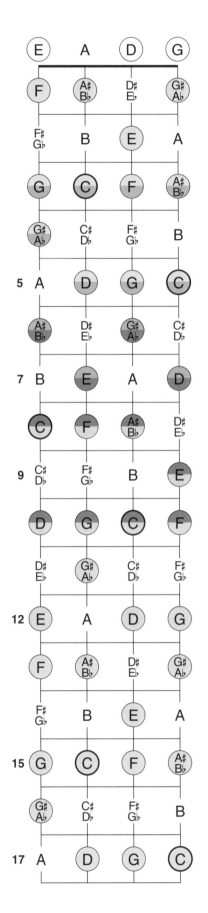

C♯ MIXOLYDIAN ♭6

C♯–D♯–E♯–F♯–G♯–A–B

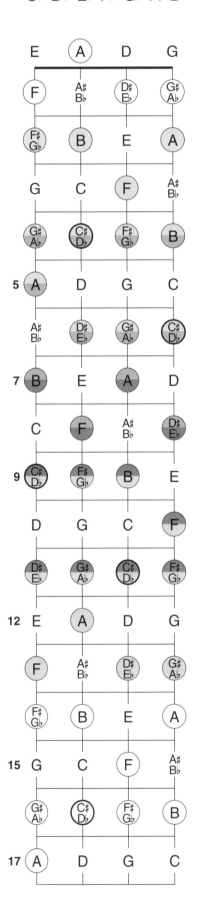

D MIXOLYDIAN ♭6

D–E–F♯–G–A–B♭–C

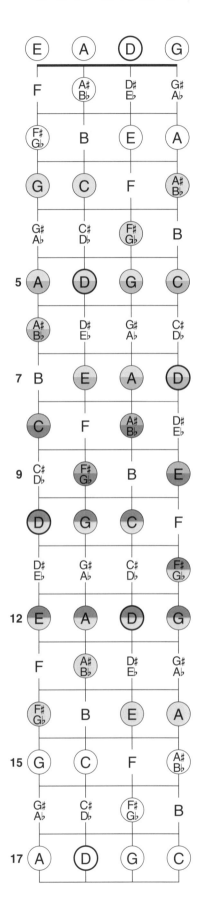

E♭ MIXOLYDIAN ♭6

E♭–F–G–A♭–B♭–C♭–D♭

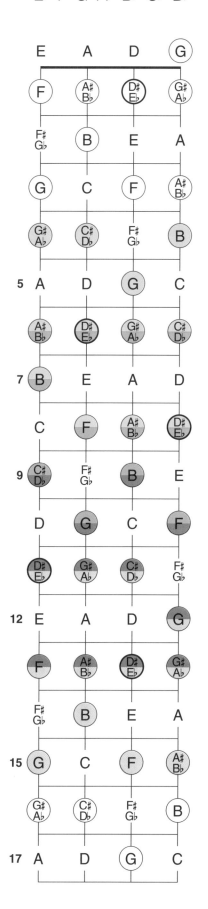

E MIXOLYDIAN ♭6

E–F♯–G♯–A–B–C–D

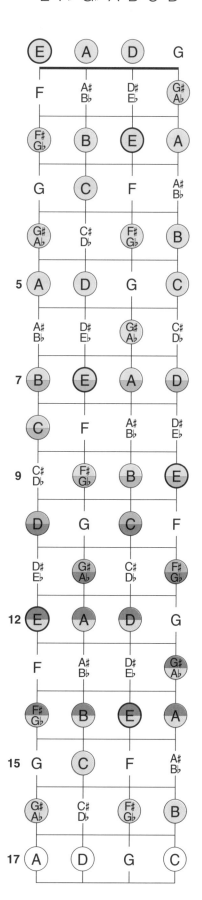

F MIXOLYDIAN ♭6

F–G–A–B♭–C–D♭–E♭

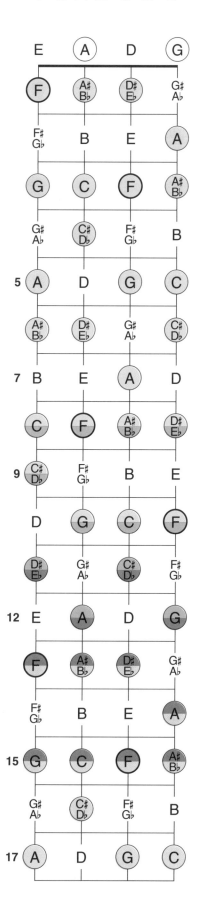

F♯ MIXOLYDIAN ♭6

F♯–G♯–A♯–B–C♯–D–E

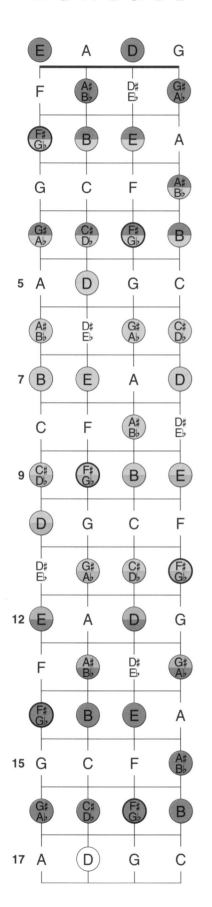

G MIXOLYDIAN ♭6

G–A–B–C–D–E♭–F

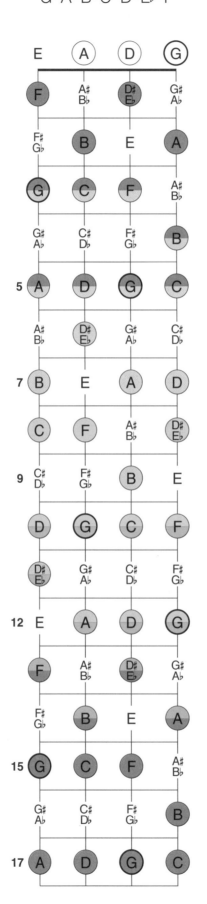

A♭ MIXOLYDIAN ♭6

A♭–B♭–C–D♭–E♭–F♭–G♭

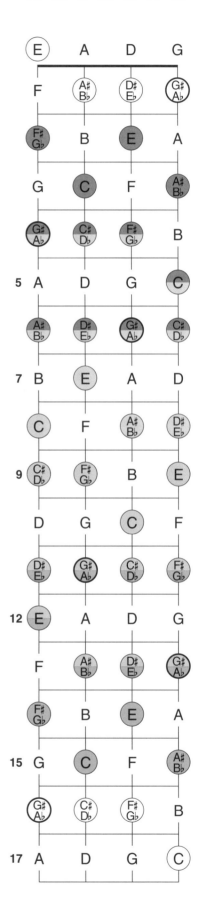

A MIXOLYDIAN ♭6

A–B–C♯–D–E–F–G

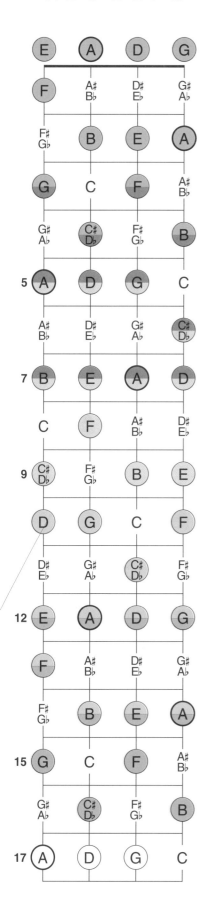

B♭ MIXOLYDIAN ♭6

B♭–C–D–E♭–F–G♭–A♭

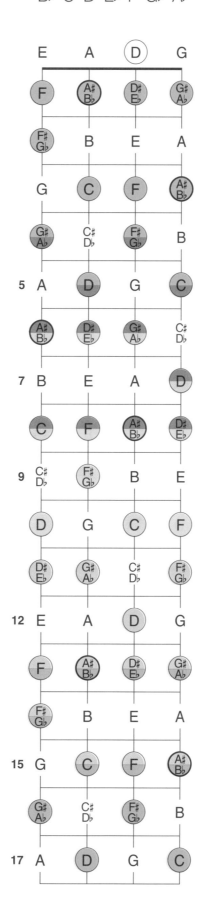

B MIXOLYDIAN ♭6

B–C♯–D♯–E–F♯–G–A

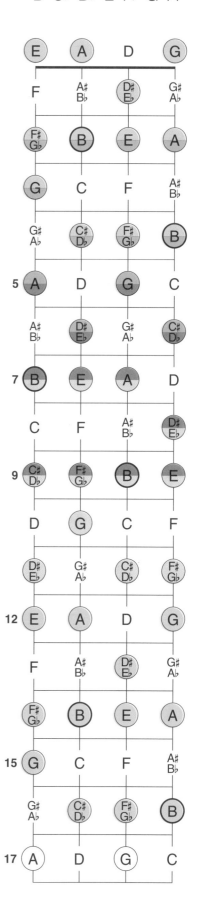

71

C LOCRIAN ♮2

C–D–E♭–F–G♭–A♭–B♭

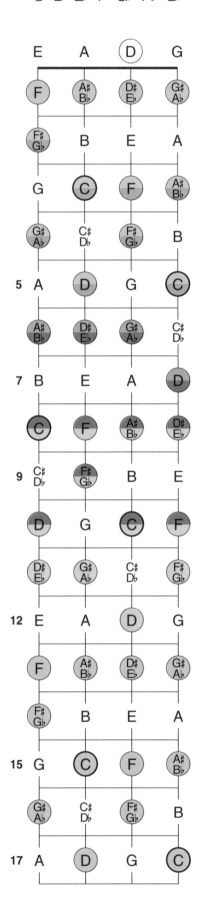

C♯ LOCRIAN ♮2

C♯–D♯–E–F♯–G–A–B

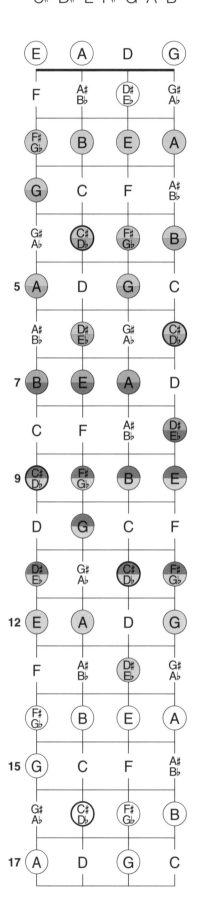

D LOCRIAN ♮2

D–E–F–G–A♭–B♭–C

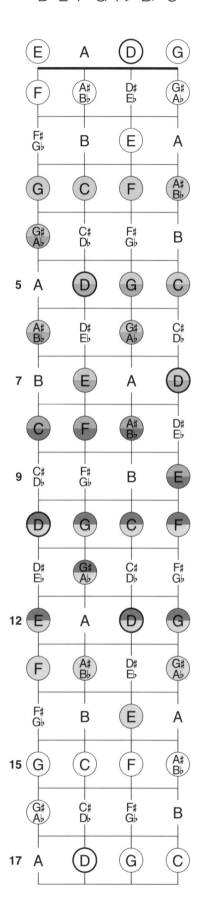

D♯ LOCRIAN ♭2

D♯–E♯–F♯–G♯–A–B–C♯

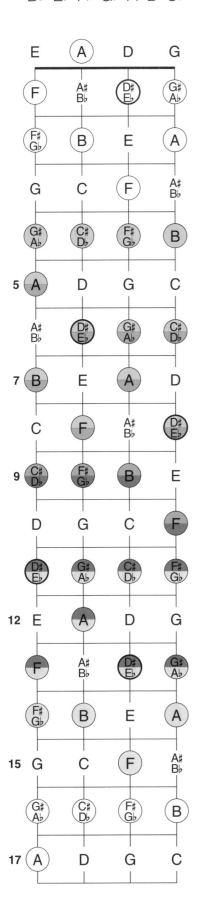

E LOCRIAN ♭2

E–F♯–G–A–B♭–C–D

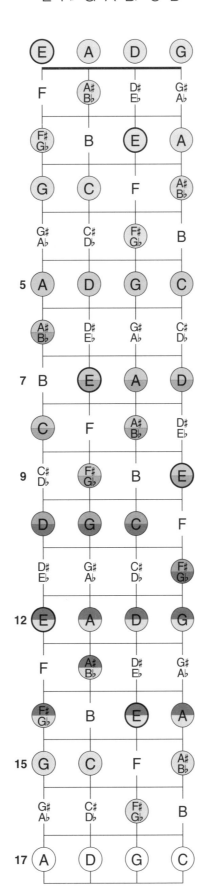

F LOCRIAN ♭2

F–G–A♭–B♭–C♭–D♭–E♭

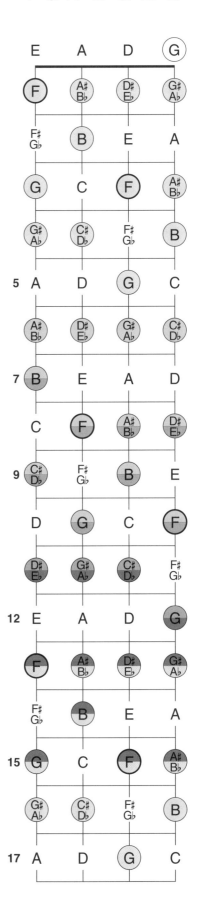

F# LOCRIAN ♭2

F#–G#–A–B–C–D–E

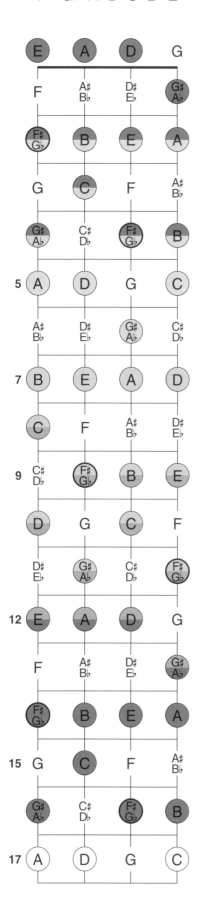

G LOCRIAN ♭2

G–A–B♭–C–D♭–E♭–F

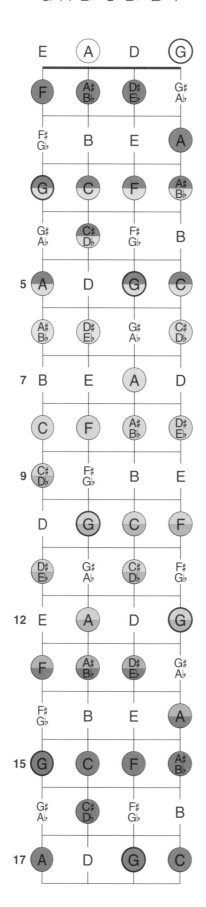

G# LOCRIAN ♭2

G#–A#–B–C#–D–E–F#

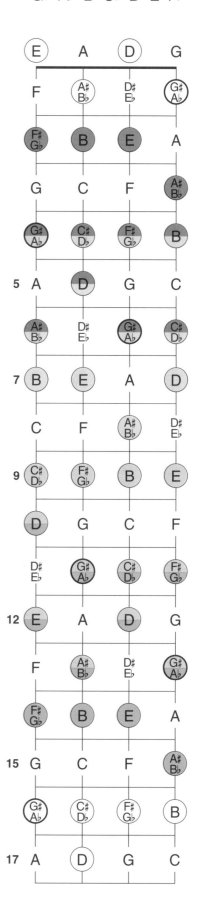

A LOCRIAN ♮2

A–B–C–D–E♭–F–G

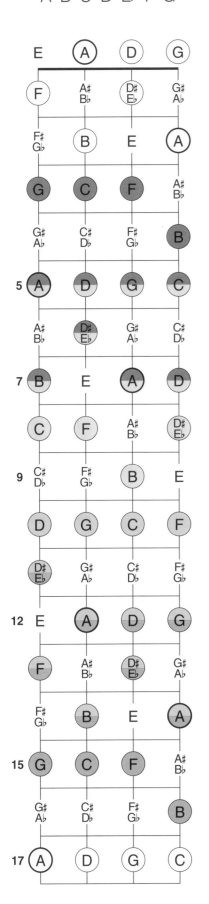

B♭ LOCRIAN ♮2

B♭–C–D♭–E♭–F♭–G♭–A♭

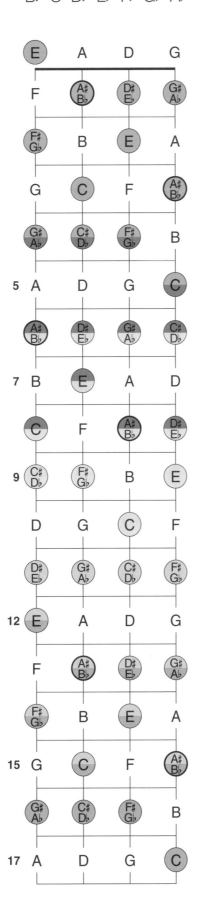

B LOCRIAN ♮2

B–C♯–D–E–F–G–A

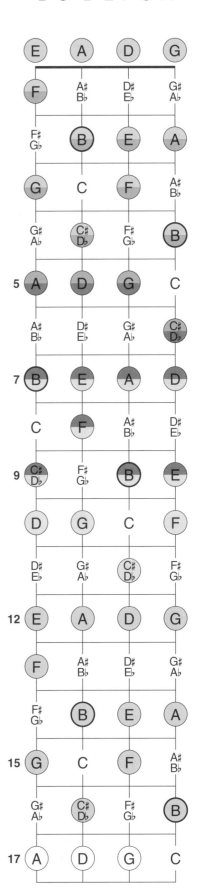

C SUPER LOCRIAN

C–Db–Eb–Fb–Gb–Ab–Bb

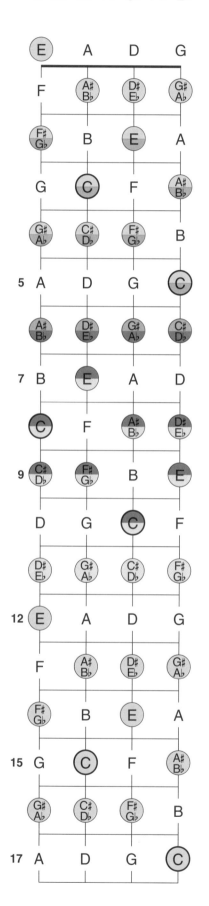

C# SUPER LOCRIAN

C#–D–E–F–G–A–B

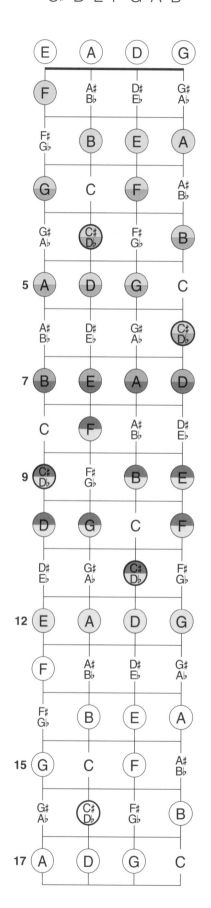

D SUPER LOCRIAN

D–Eb–F–Gb–Ab–Bb–C

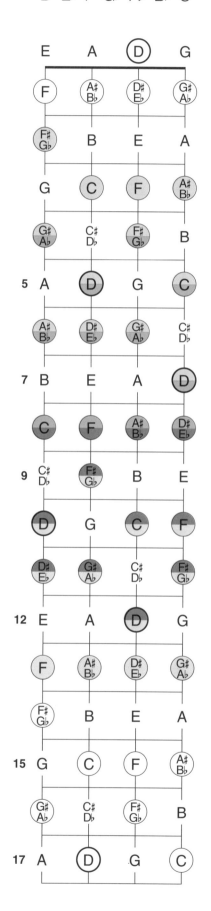

D♯ SUPER LOCRIAN

D♯–E–F♯–G–A–B–C♯

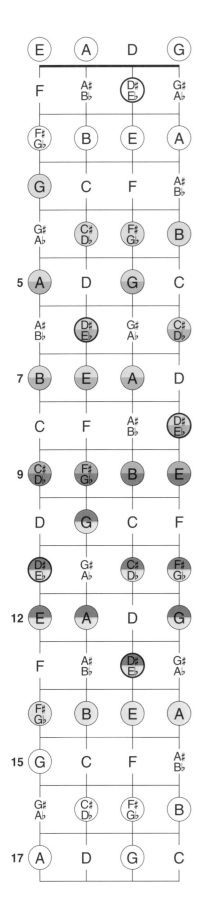

E SUPER LOCRIAN

E–F–G–A♭–B♭–C–D

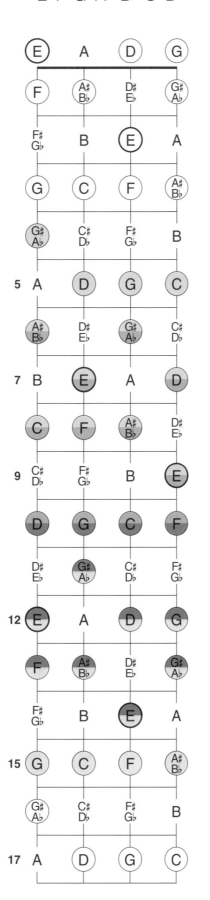

F SUPER LOCRIAN

F–G♭–A♭–B♭♭–C♭–D♭–E♭

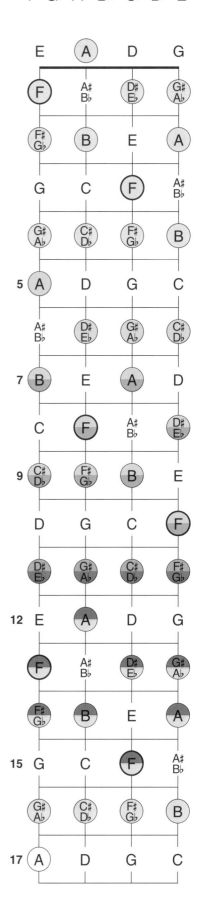

F♯ SUPER LOCRIAN

F♯–G–A–B♭–C–D–E

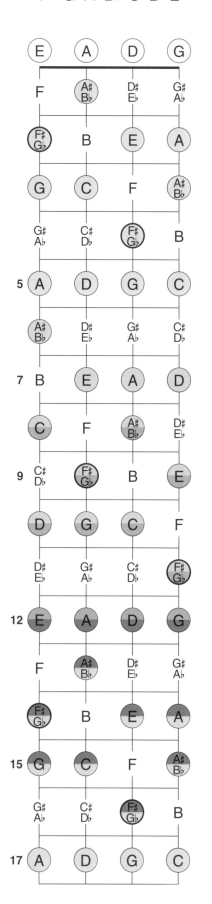

G SUPER LOCRIAN

G–A♭–B♭–C♭–D♭–E♭–F

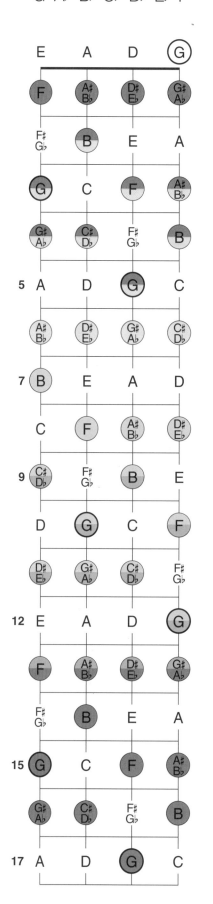

G♯ SUPER LOCRIAN

G♯–A–B–C–D–E–F♯

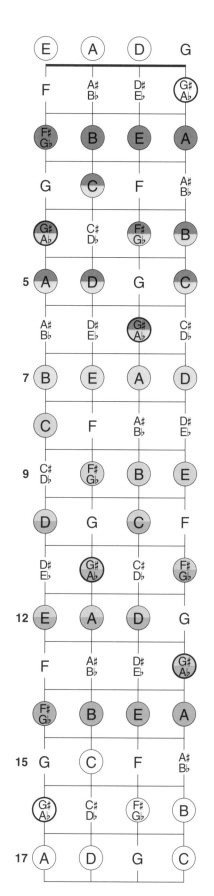

A SUPER LOCRIAN

A–B♭–C–D♭–E♭–F–G

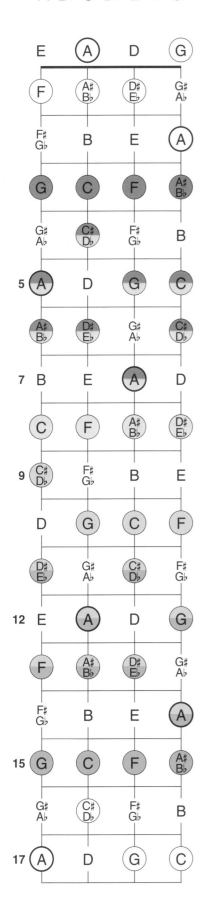

A♯ SUPER LOCRIAN

A♯–B–C♯–D–E–F♯–G♯

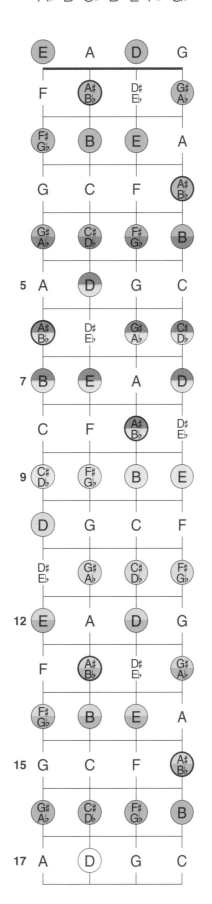

B SUPER LOCRIAN

B–C–D–E♭–F–G–A

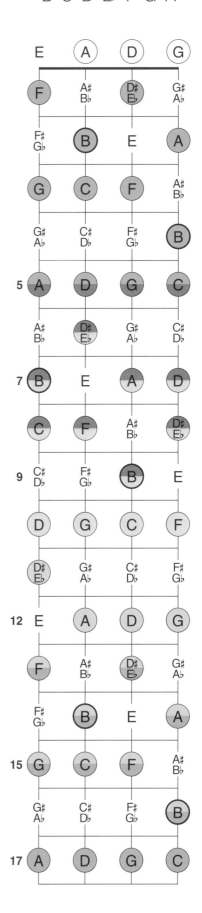

SCALES

THE HARMONIC MINOR SCALE AND ITS MODES

C HARMONIC MINOR

C–D–E♭–F–G–A♭–B

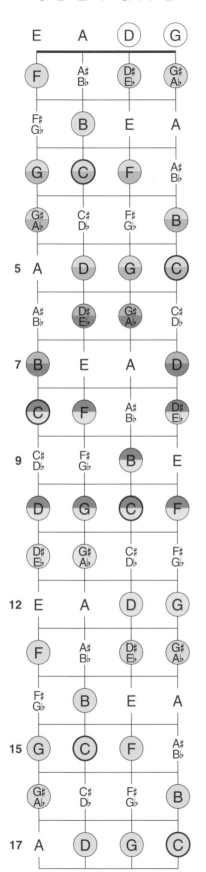

C# HARMONIC MINOR

C#–D#–E–F#–G#–A–B#

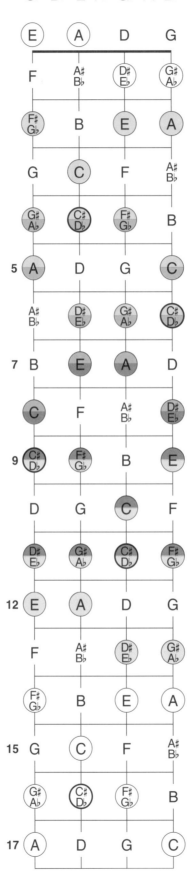

D HARMONIC MINOR

D–E–F–G–A–B♭–C#

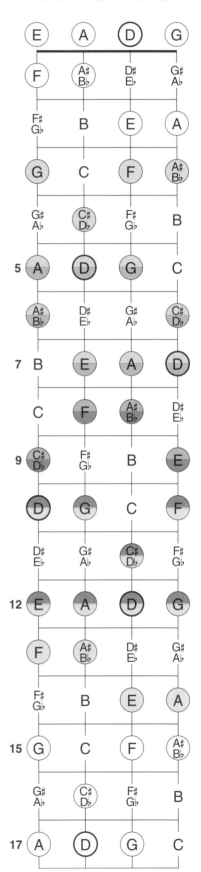

E♭ HARMONIC MINOR

E♭–F–G♭–A♭–B♭–C♭–D

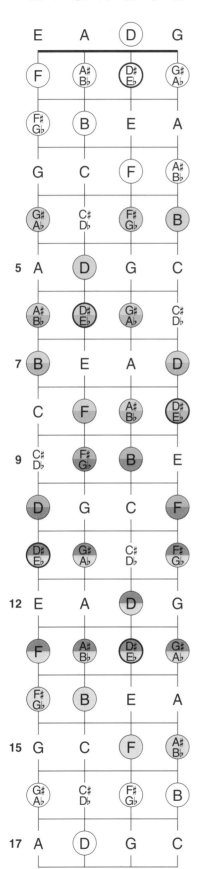

E HARMONIC MINOR

E–F#–G–A–B–C–D#

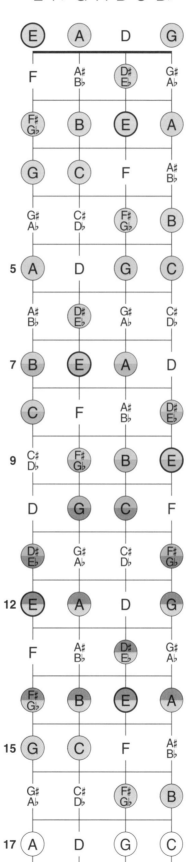

F HARMONIC MINOR

F–G–A♭–B♭–C–D♭–E

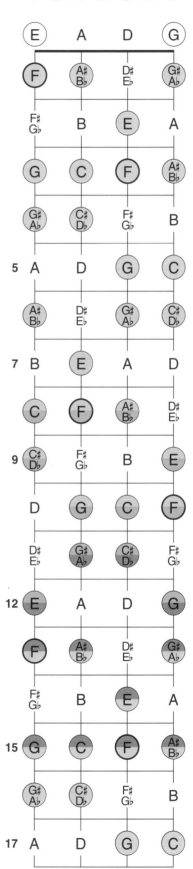

F♯ HARMONIC MINOR

F♯–G♯–A–B–C♯–D–E♯

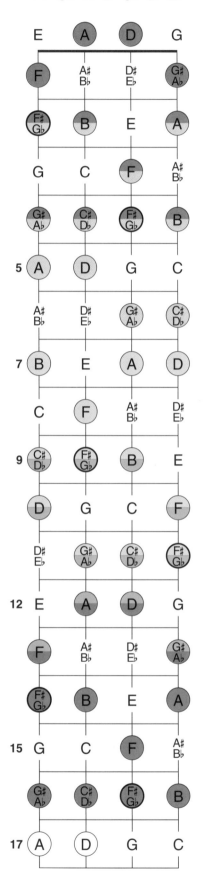

G HARMONIC MINOR

G–A–B♭–C–D–E♭–F♯

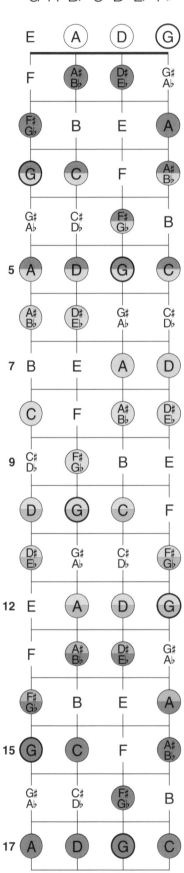

A♭ HARMONIC MINOR

A♭–B♭–C♭–D♭–E♭–F♭–G

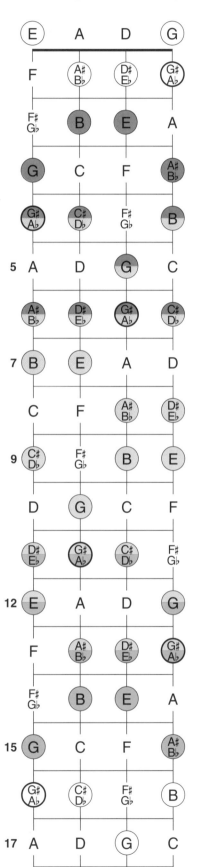

A HARMONIC MINOR

A–B–C–D–E–F–G#

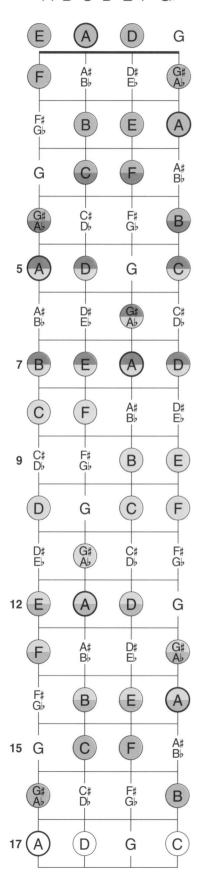

B♭ HARMONIC MINOR

B♭–C–D♭–E♭–F–G♭–A

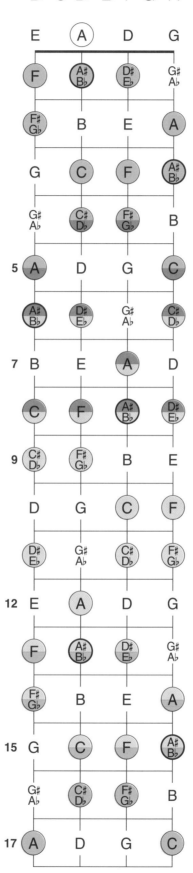

B HARMONIC MINOR

B–C#–D–E–F#–G–A#

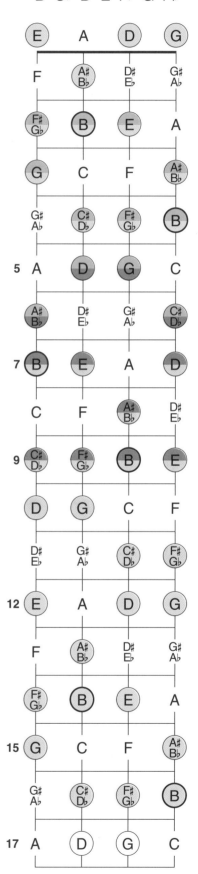

C LOCRIAN ♮6

C–D♭–E♭–F–G♭–A–B♭

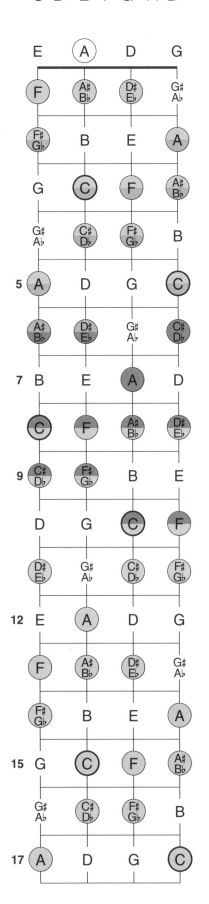

C♯ LOCRIAN ♮6

C♯–D–E–F♯–G–A♯–B

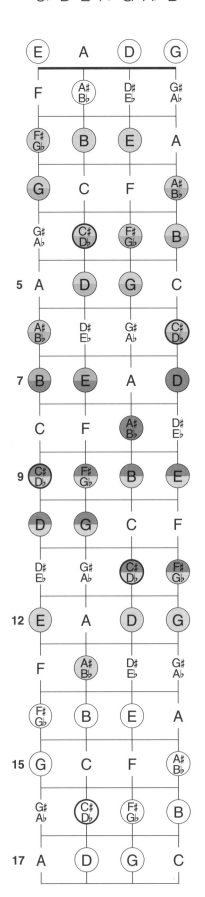

D LOCRIAN ♮6

D–E♭–F–G–A♭–B–C

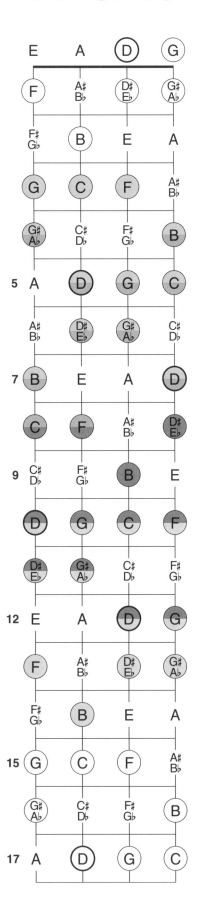

D♯ LOCRIAN ♮6

D♯–E–F♯–G♯–A–B♯–C♯

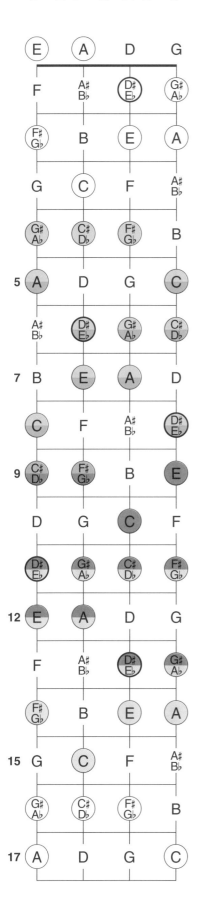

E LOCRIAN ♮6

E–F–G–A–B♭–C♯–D

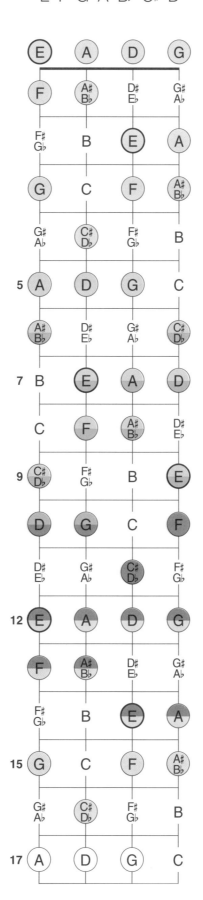

F LOCRIAN ♮6

F–G♭–A♭–B♭–C♭–D–E♭

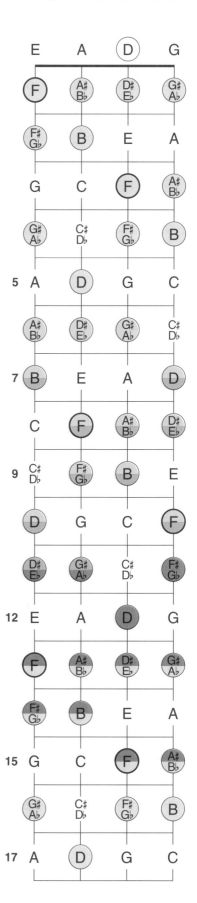

F# LOCRIAN ♮6

F#–G–A–B–C–D#–E

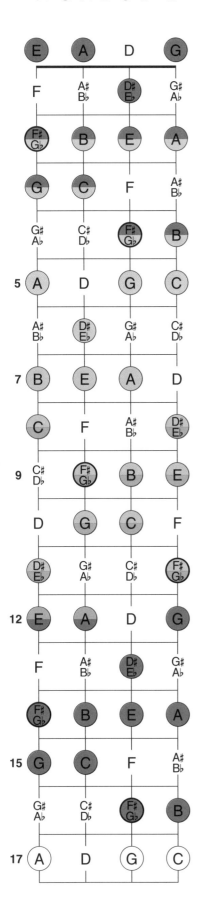

G LOCRIAN ♮6

G–A♭–B♭–C–D♭–E–F

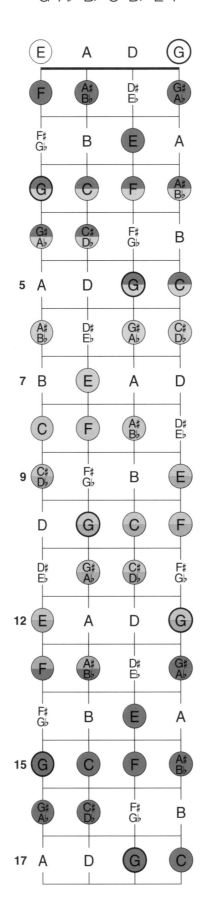

G# LOCRIAN ♮6

G#–A–B–C#–D–E#–F#

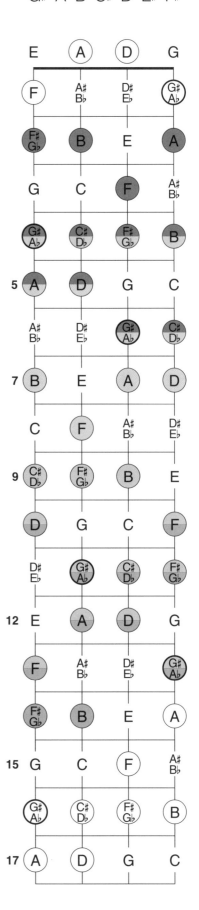

A LOCRIAN ♮6

A–B♭–C–D–E♭–F♯–G

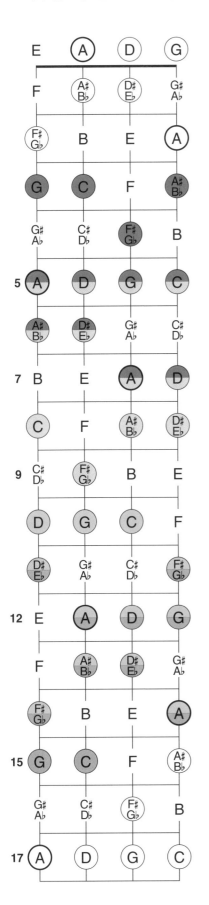

A♯ LOCRIAN ♮6

A♯–B–C♯–D♯–E–F𝄪–G♯

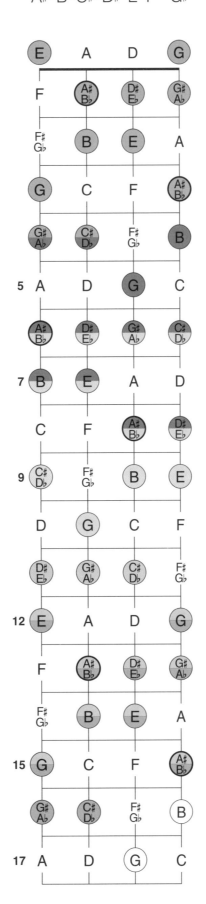

B LOCRIAN ♮6

B–C–D–E–F–G♯–A

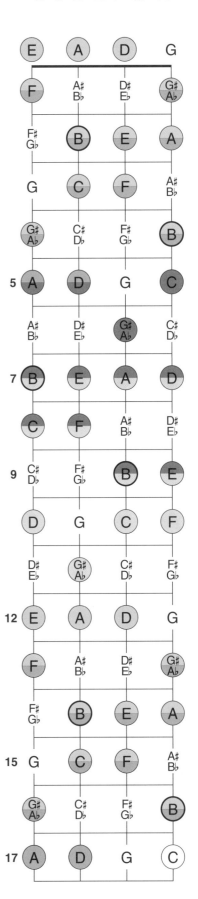

C IONIAN #5

C–D–E–F–G#–A–B

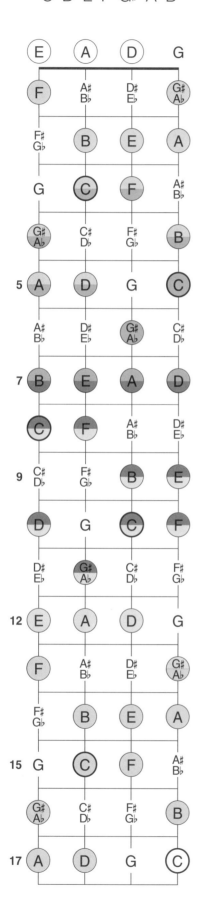

Db IONIAN #5

Db–Eb–F–Gb–A–Bb–C

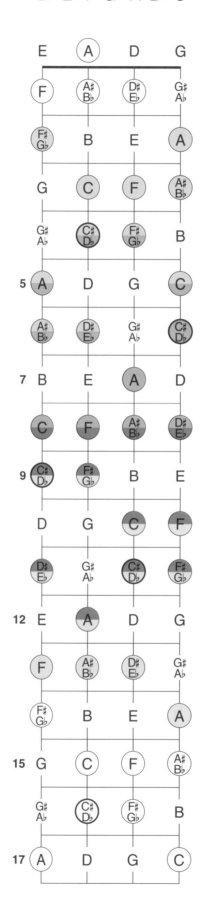

D IONIAN #5

D–E–F#–G–A#–B–C#

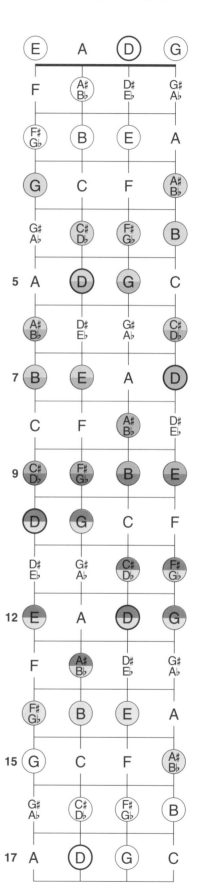

Eb IONIAN #5

Eb–F–G–Ab–B–C–D

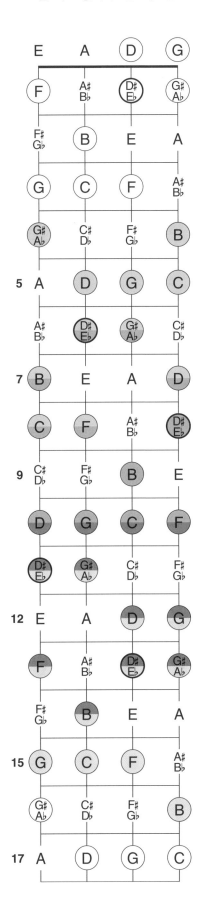

E IONIAN #5

E–F#–G#–A–B#–C#–D#

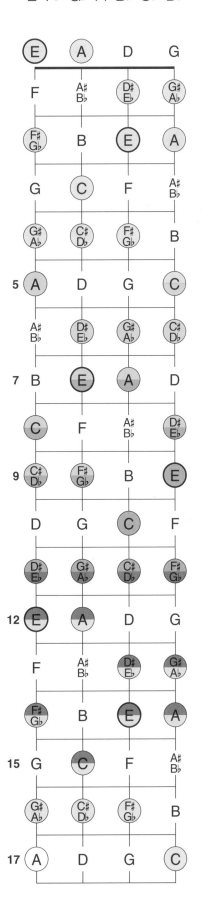

F IONIAN #5

F–G–A–Bb–C#–D–E

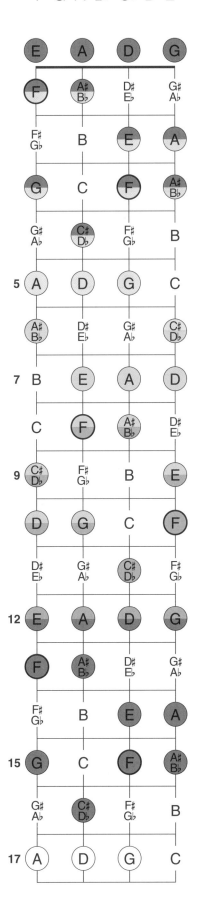

G♭ IONIAN #5

G♭–A♭–B♭–C♭–D–E♭–F

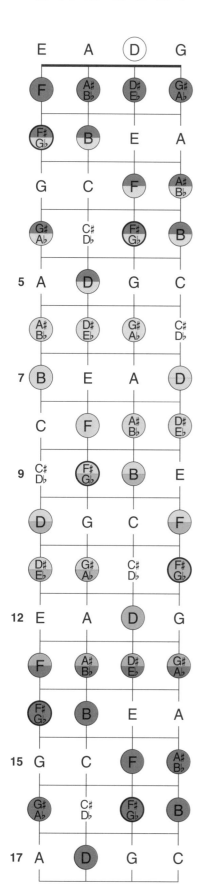

G IONIAN #5

G–A–B–C–D#–E–F#

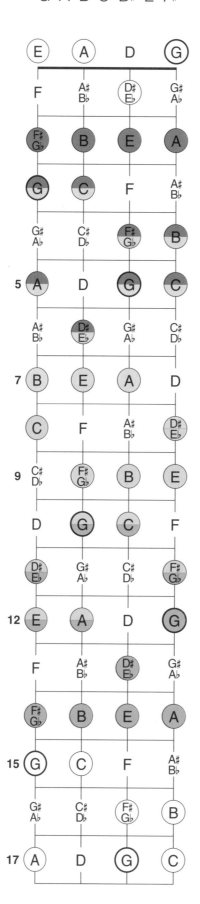

A♭ IONIAN #5

A♭–B♭–C–D♭–E–F–G

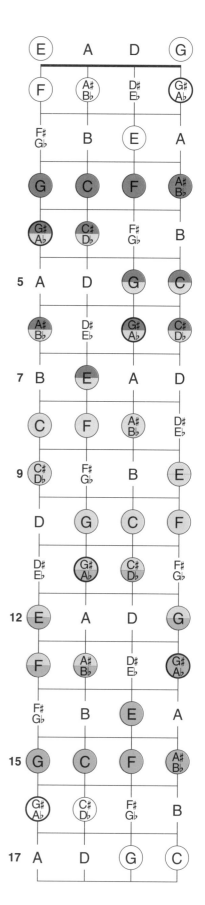

A IONIAN ♯5

A–B–C♯–D–E♯–F♯–G♯

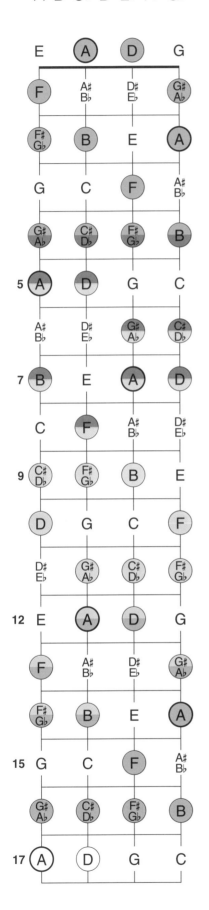

B♭ IONIAN ♯5

B♭–C–D–E♭–F♯–G–A

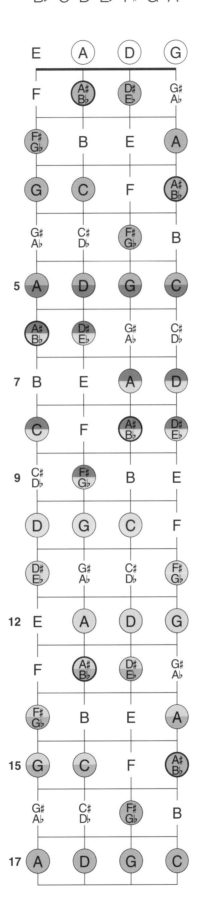

B IONIAN ♯5

B–C♯–D♯–E–F𝄪–G♯–A♯

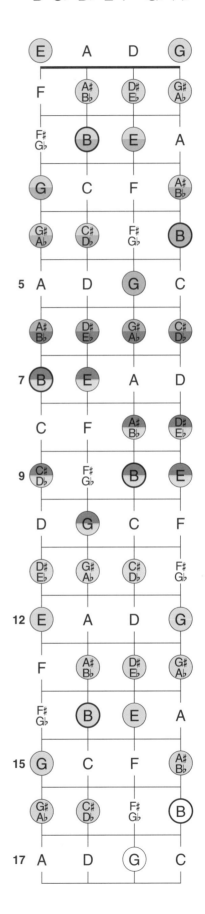

C DORIAN #4

C–D–E♭–F#–G–A–B♭

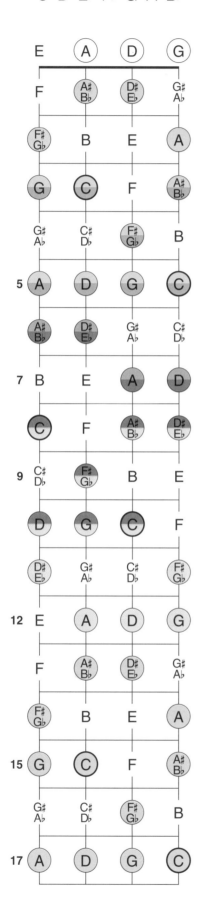

D♭ DORIAN #4

D♭–E♭–F♭–G–A♭–B♭–C♭

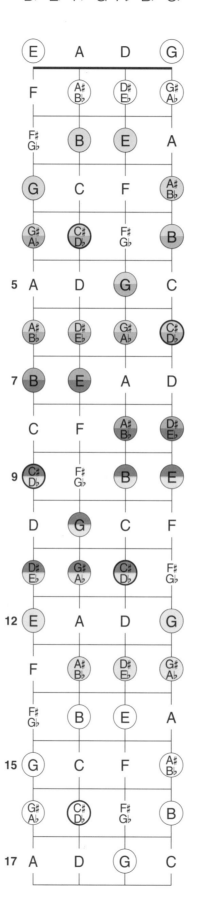

D DORIAN #4

D–E–F–G#–A–B–C

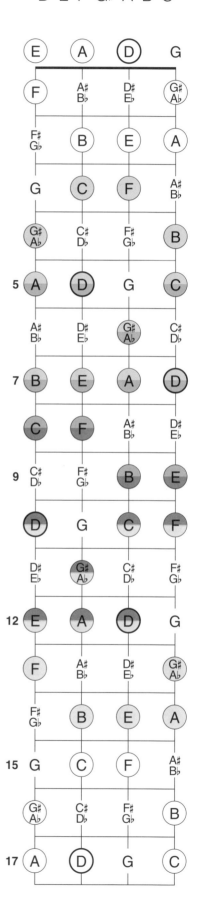

E♭ DORIAN ♯4

E♭–F–G♭–A–B♭–C–D♭

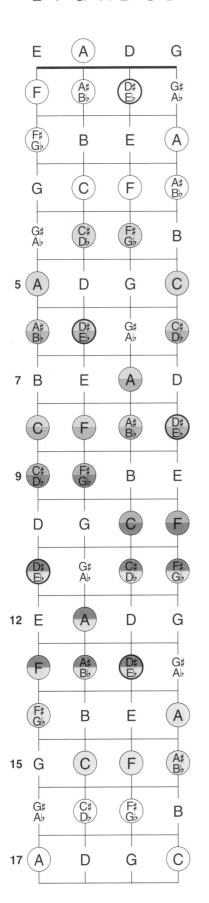

E DORIAN ♯4

E–F♯–G–A♯–B–C♯–D

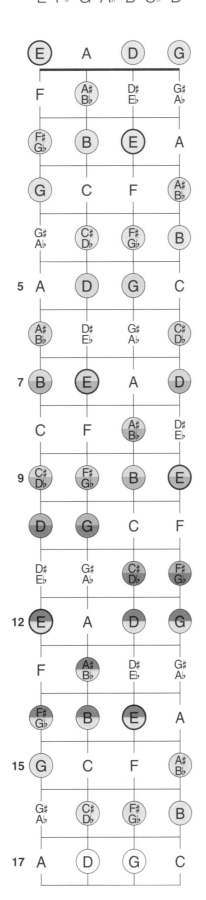

F DORIAN ♯4

F–G–A♭–B–C–D–E♭

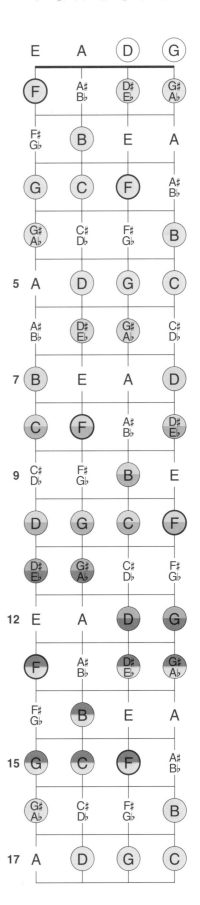

F# DORIAN #4

F#–G#–A–B#–C#–D#–E

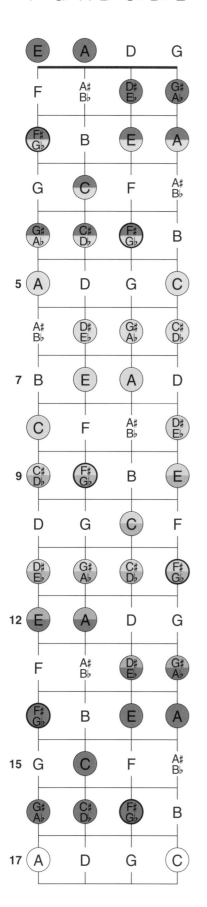

G DORIAN #4

G–A–B♭–C#–D–E–F

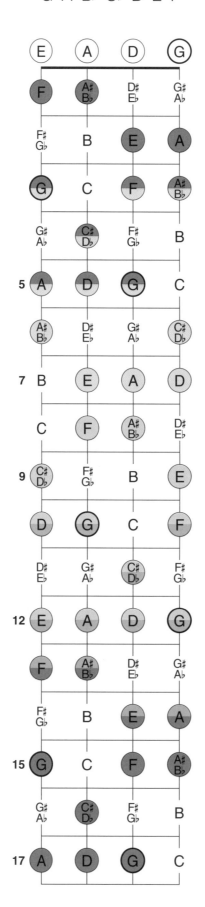

A♭ DORIAN #4

A♭–B♭–C♭–D–E♭–F–G♭

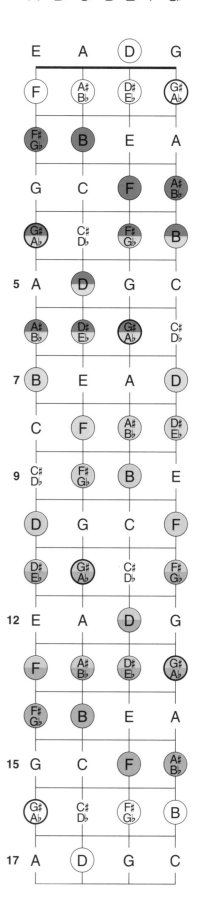

A DORIAN #4

A–B–C–D#–E–F#–G

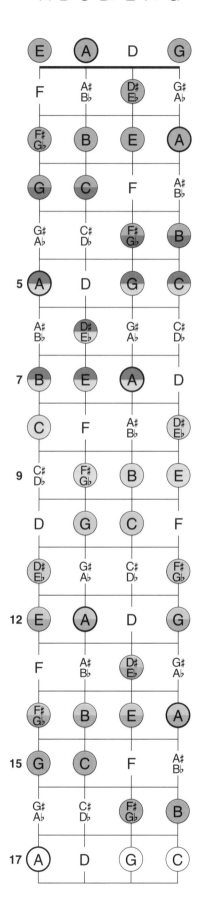

Bb DORIAN #4

Bb–C–Db–E–F–G–Ab

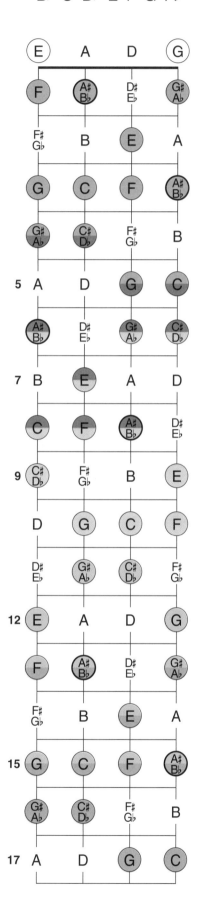

B DORIAN #4

B–C#–D–E#–F#–G#–A

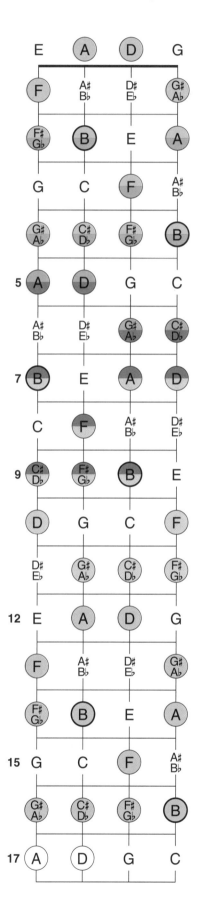

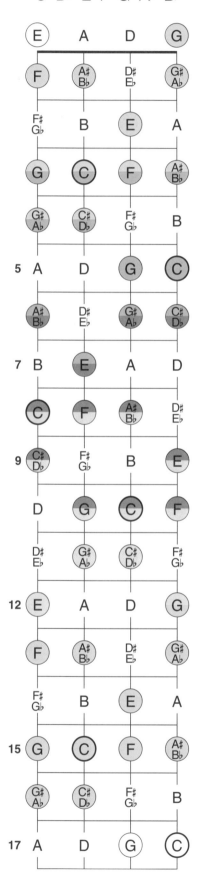

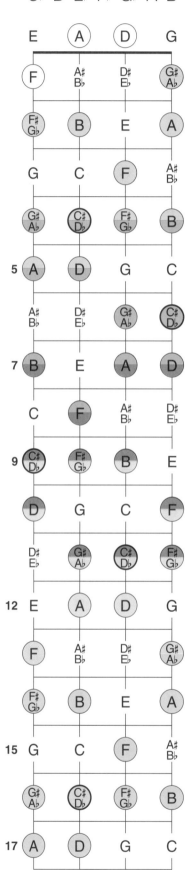

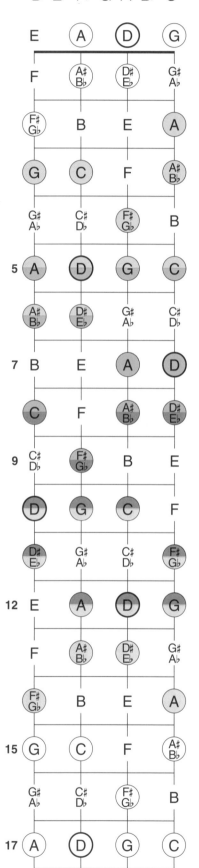

C PHRYGIAN DOMINANT

C–D♭–E–F–G–A♭–B♭

C♯ PHRYGIAN DOMINANT

C♯–D–E♯–F♯–G♯–A–B

D PHRYGIAN DOMINANT

D–E♭–F♯–G–A–B♭–C

E♭ PHRYGIAN DOMINANT

E♭–F♭–G–A♭–B♭–C♭–D♭

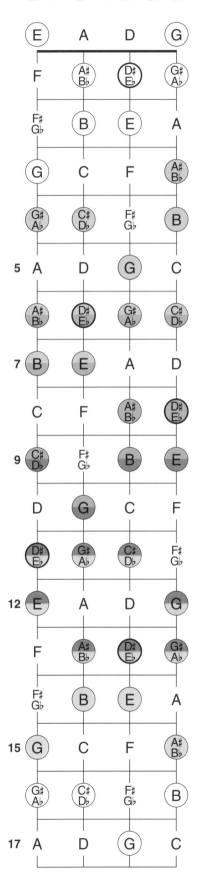

E PHRYGIAN DOMINANT

E–F–G#–A–B–C–D

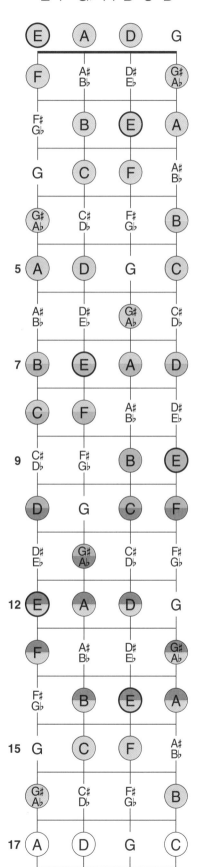

F PHRYGIAN DOMINANT

F–G♭–A–B♭–C–D♭–E♭

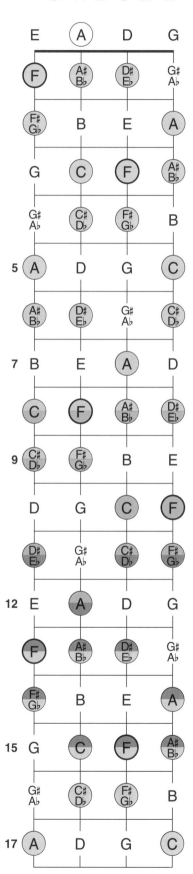

F♯ PHRYGIAN DOMINANT

F♯–G–A♯–B–C♯–D–E

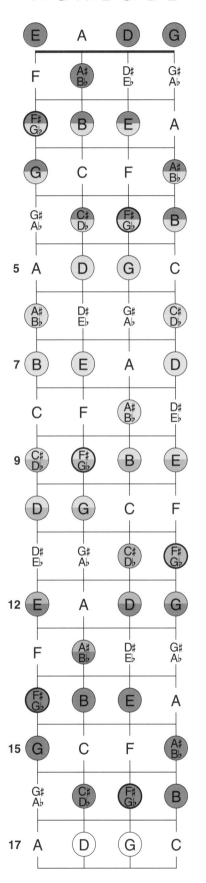

G PHRYGIAN DOMINANT

G–A♭–B–C–D–E♭–F

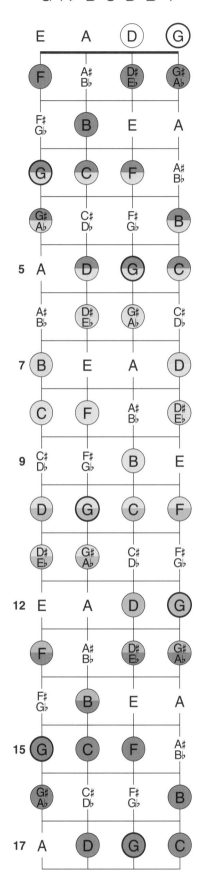

G♯ PHRYGIAN DOMINANT

G♯–A–B♯–C♯–D♯–E–F♯

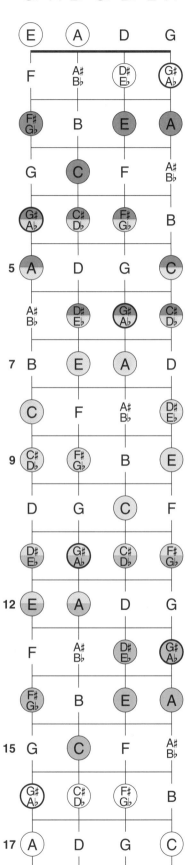

A PHRYGIAN DOMINANT

A–B♭–C♯–D–E–F–G

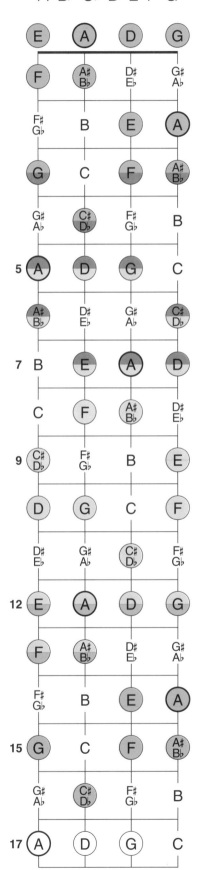

B♭ PHRYGIAN DOMINANT

B♭–C♭–D–E♭–F–G♭–A♭

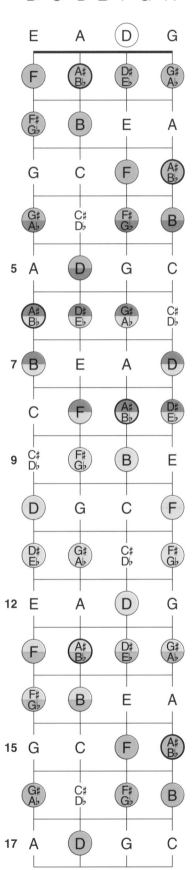

B PHRYGIAN DOMINANT

B–C–D♯–E–F♯–G–A

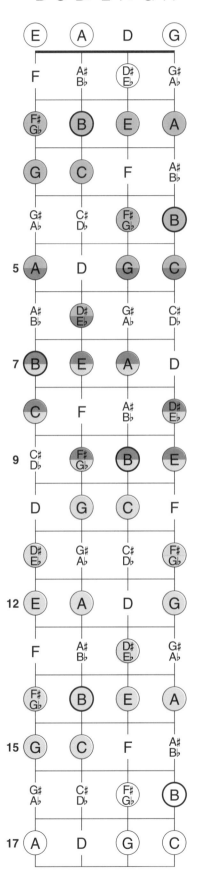

C LYDIAN #2

C–D#–E–F#–G–A–B

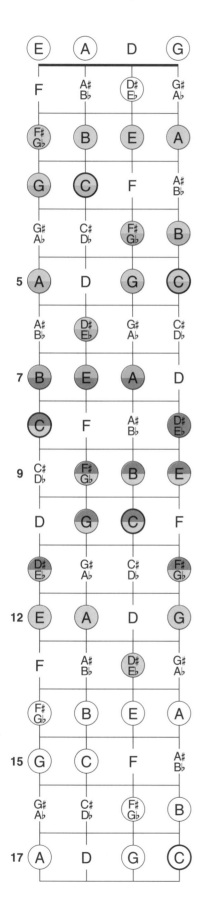

Db LYDIAN #2

Db–E–F–G–Ab–Bb–C

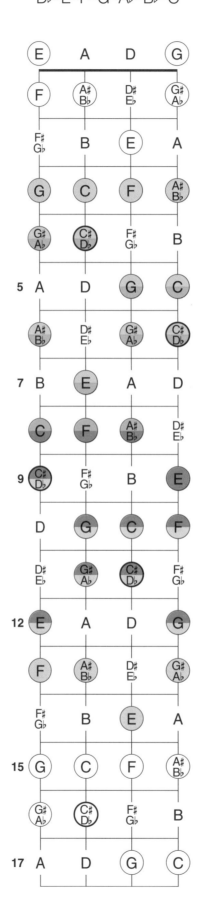

D LYDIAN #2

D–E#–F#–G#–A–B–C#

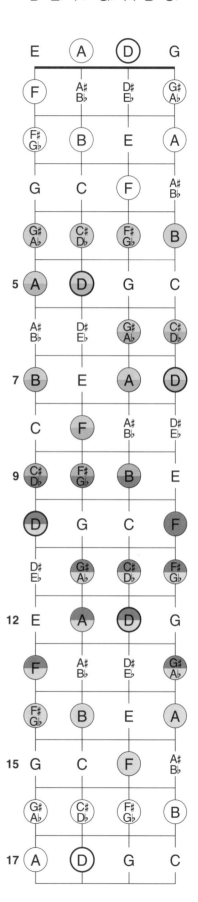

E♭ LYDIAN ♯2

E♭–F♯–G–A–B♭–C–D

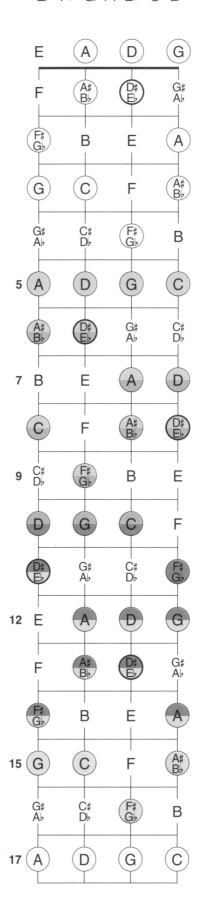

E♭ LYDIAN ♯2

E LYDIAN ♯2

E–F𝄪–G♯–A♯–B–C♯–D♯

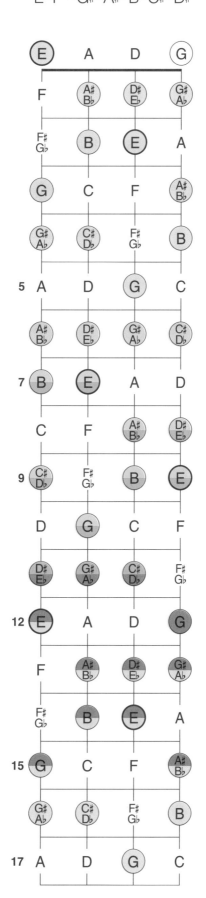

F LYDIAN ♯2

F–G♯–A–B–C–D–E

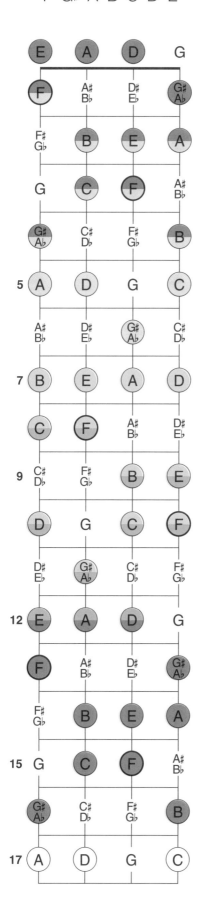

Gb LYDIAN #2

Gb–A–Bb–C–Db–Eb–F

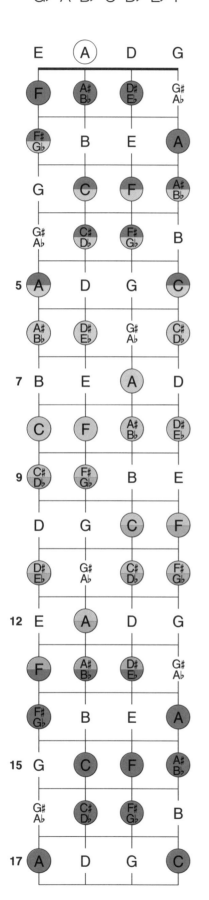

G LYDIAN #2

G–A#–B–C#–D–E–F#

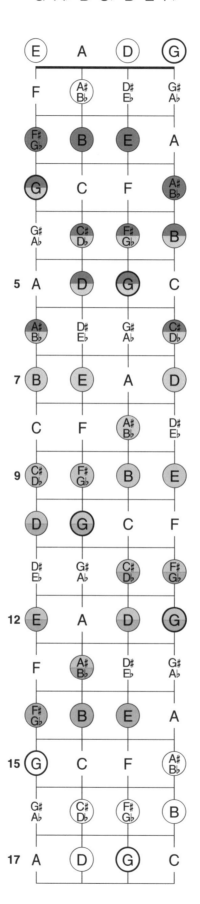

Ab LYDIAN #2

Ab–B–C–D–Eb–F–G

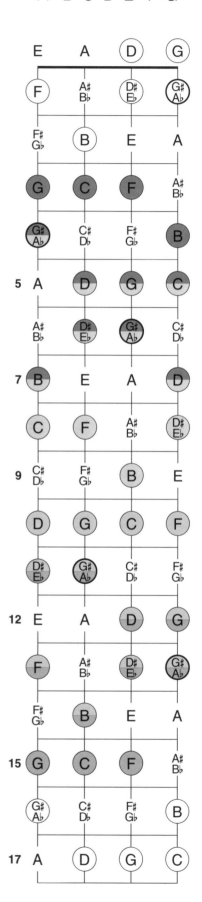

A LYDIAN #2

A–B#–C#–D#–E–F#–G#

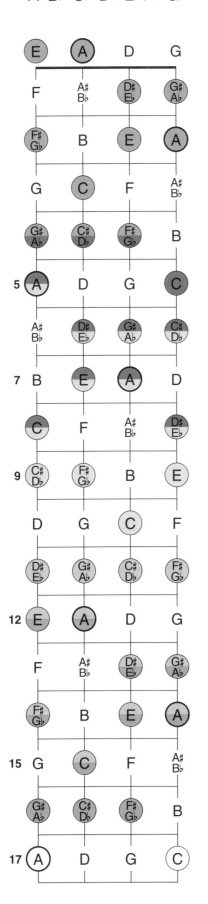

B♭ LYDIAN #2

B♭–C#–D–E–F–G–A

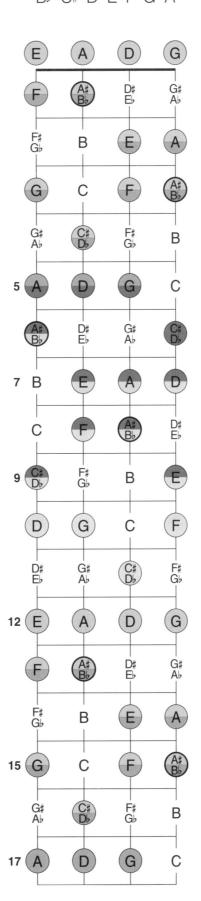

B LYDIAN #2

B–C⤫–D#–E#–F#–G#–A#

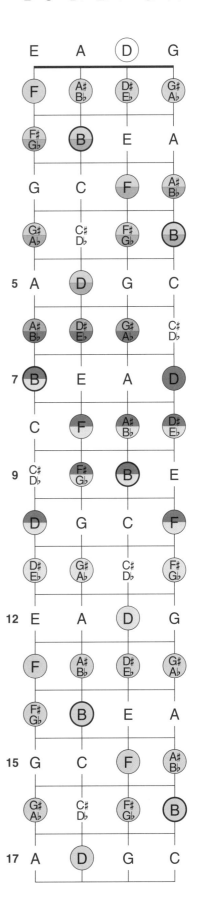

C SUPER LOCRIAN ♭♭7

C–D♭–E♭–F♭–G♭–A♭–B♭♭

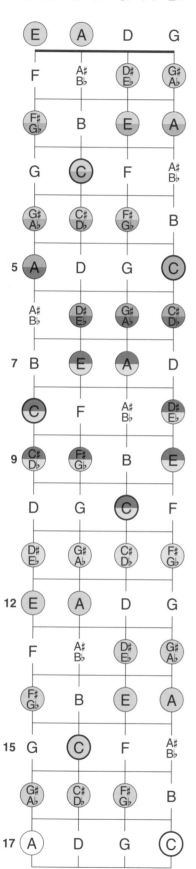

C♯ SUPER LOCRIAN ♭♭7

C♯–D–E–F–G–A–B♭

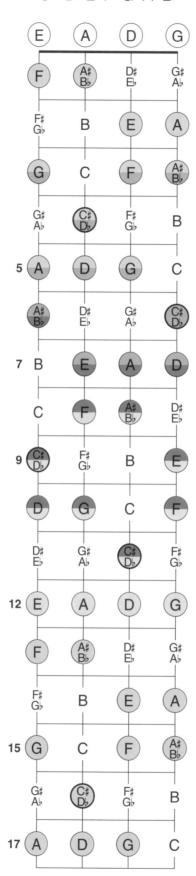

D SUPER LOCRIAN ♭♭7

D–E♭–F–G♭–A♭–B♭–C♭

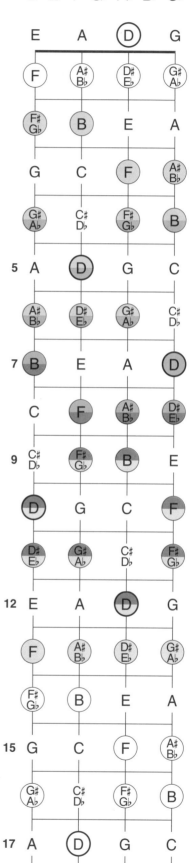

D♯ SUPER LOCRIAN ♭♭7

D♯–E–F♯–G–A–B–C

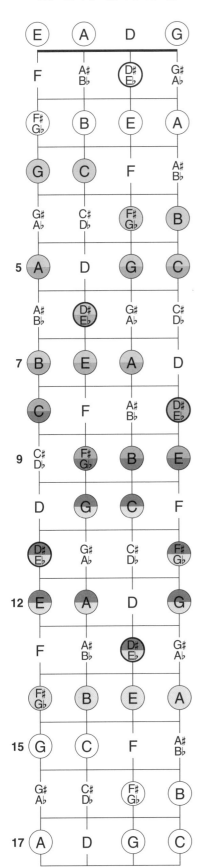

E SUPER LOCRIAN ♭♭7

E–F–G–A♭–B♭–C–D♭

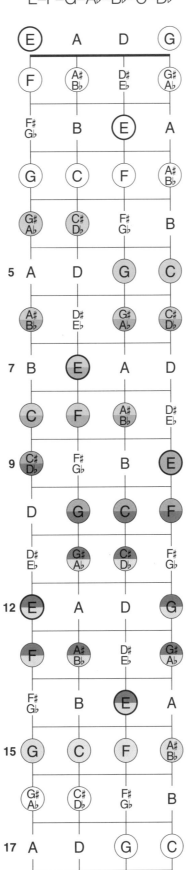

F SUPER LOCRIAN ♭♭7

F–G♭–A♭–B♭♭–C♭–D♭–E♭♭

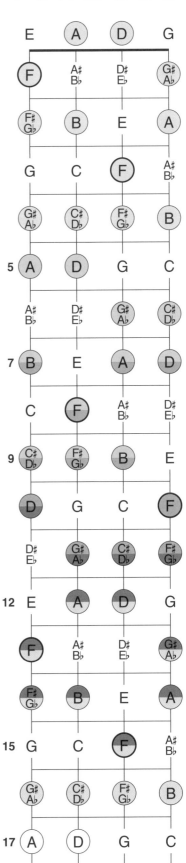

F♯ SUPER LOCRIAN ♭♭7

F♯–G–A–B♭–C–D–E♭

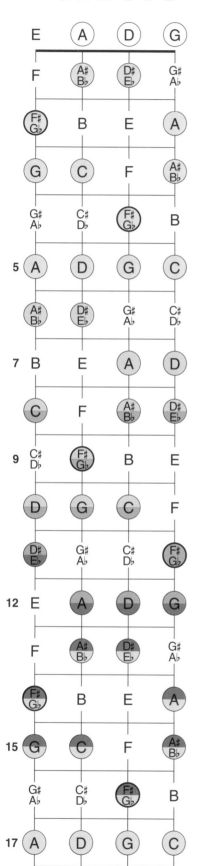

G SUPER LOCRIAN ♭♭7

G–A♭–B♭–C♭–D♭–E♭–F♭

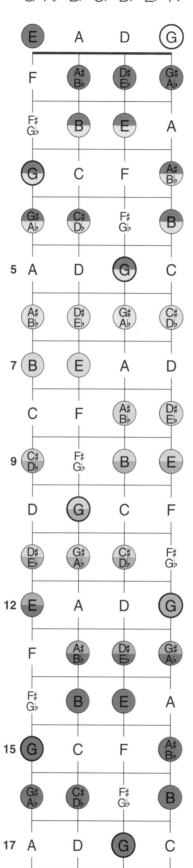

G♯ SUPER LOCRIAN ♭♭7

G♯–A–B–C–D–E–F

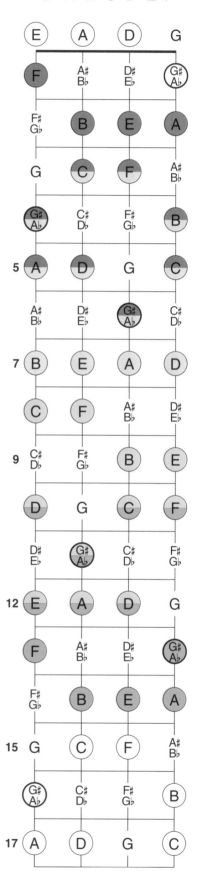

A SUPER LOCRIAN ♭♭7

A–B♭–C–D♭–E♭–F–G♭

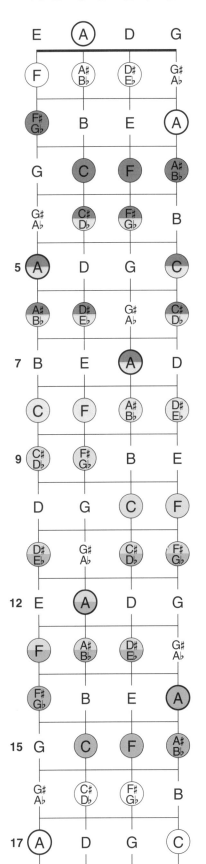

A♯ SUPER LOCRIAN ♭♭7

A♯–B–C♯–D–E–F♯–G

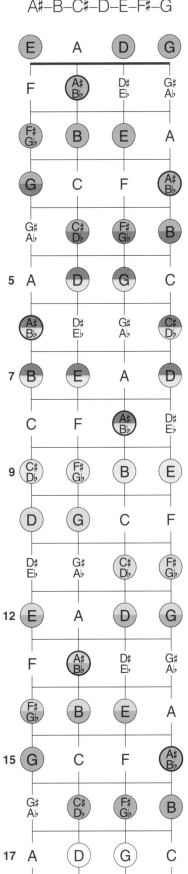

B SUPER LOCRIAN ♭♭7

B–C–D–E♭–F–G–A♭

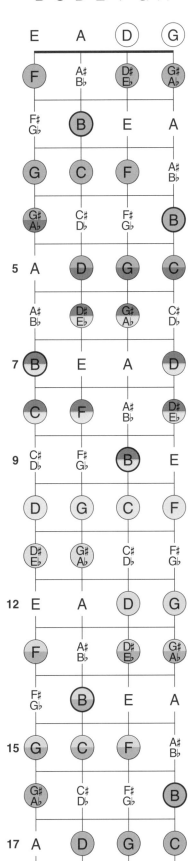

ARPEGGIOS
POWER CHORDS

C5

C–G

C#/D♭5

C#–G#/D♭–A♭

D5

D–A

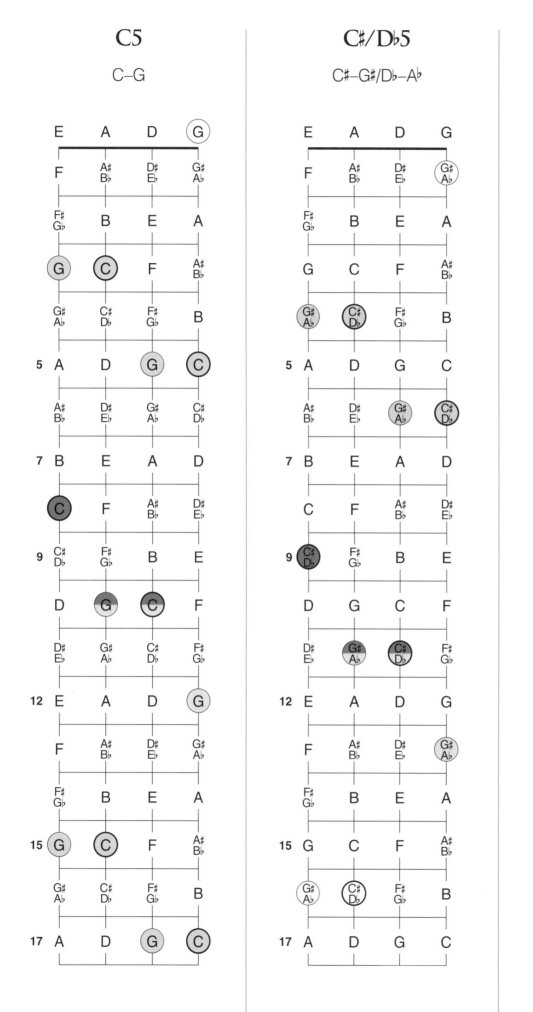

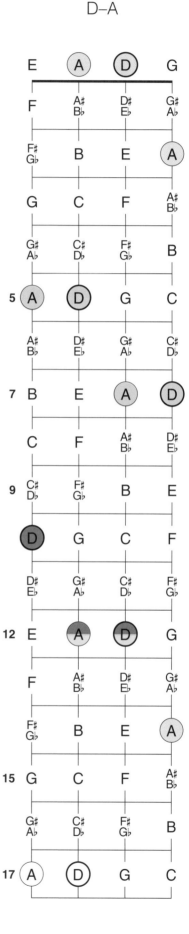

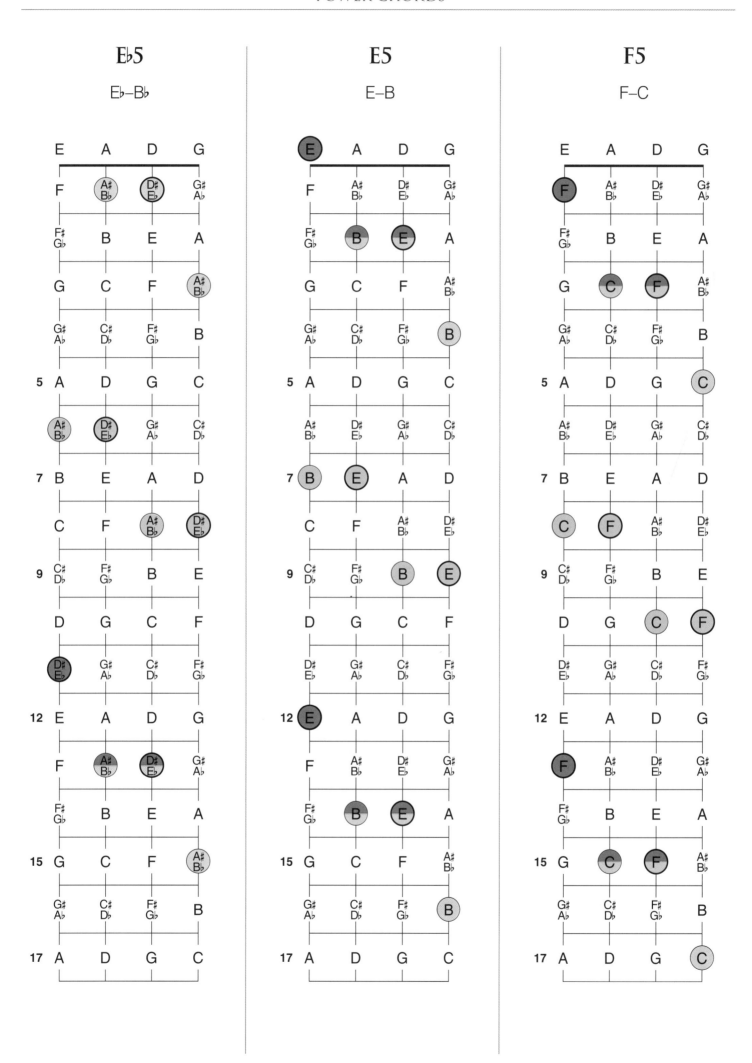

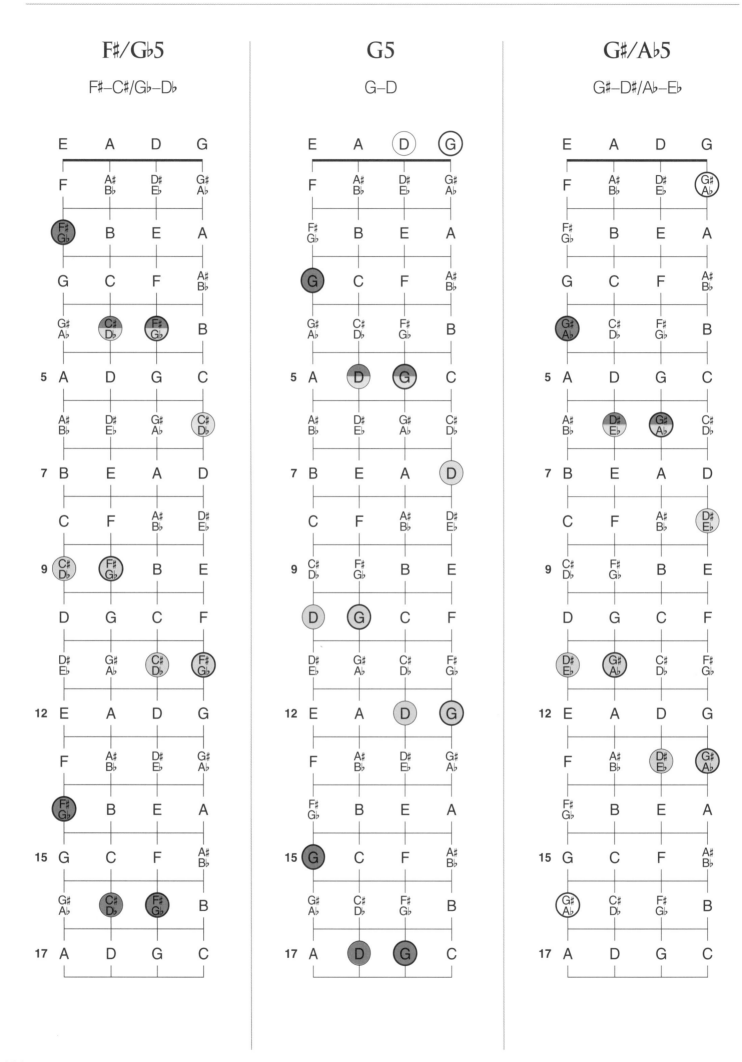

A5

A–E

B♭5

B♭–F

B5

B–F#

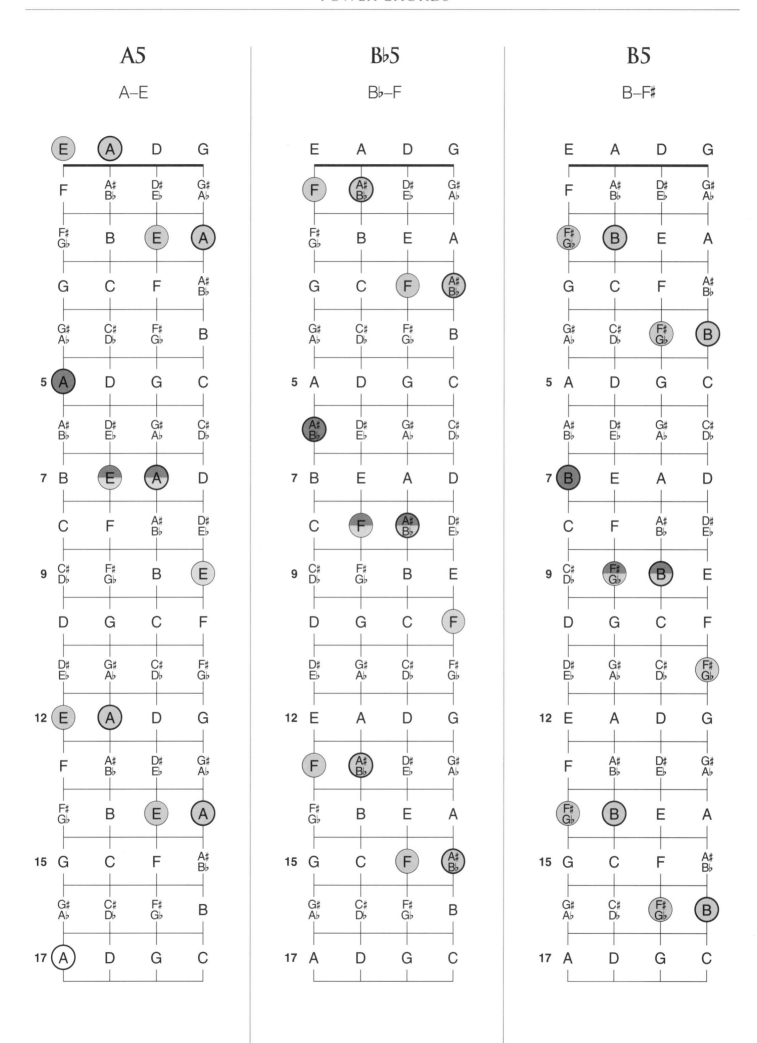

ARPEGGIOS

TRIADS

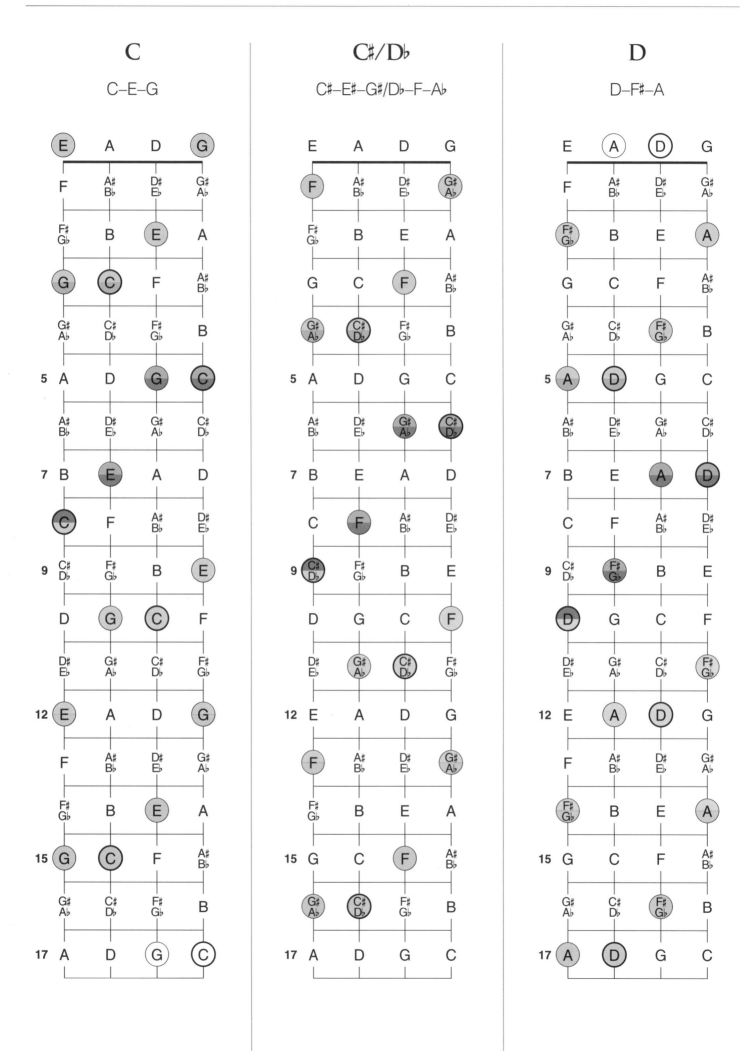

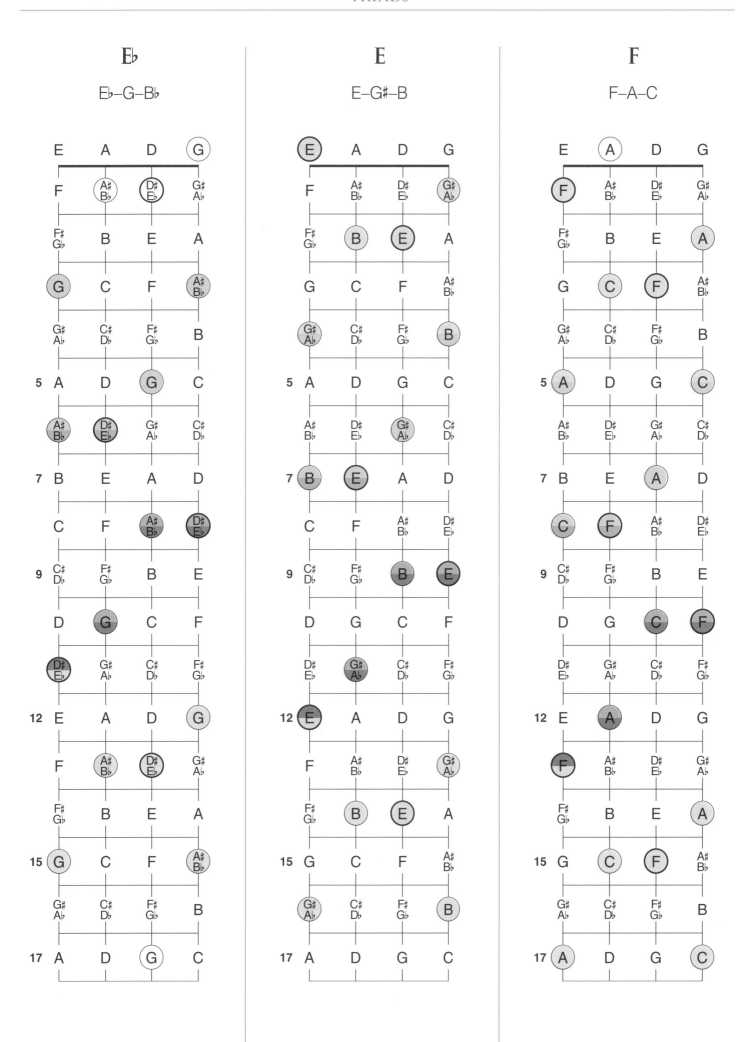

F♯/G♭

F♯–A♯–C♯/G♭–B♭–D♭

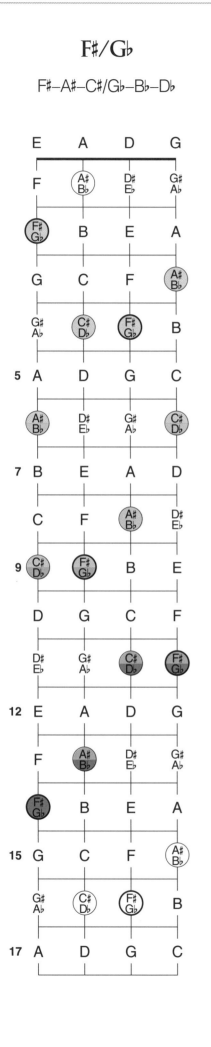

G

G–B–D

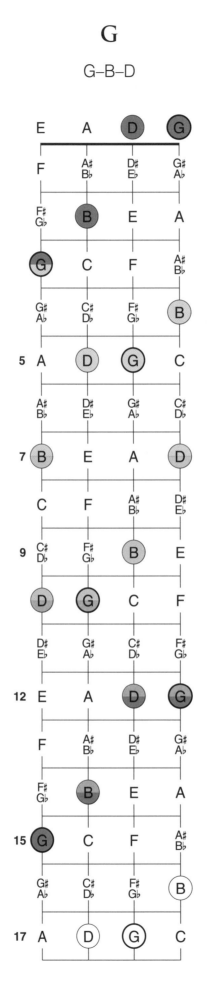

A♭

A♭–C–E♭

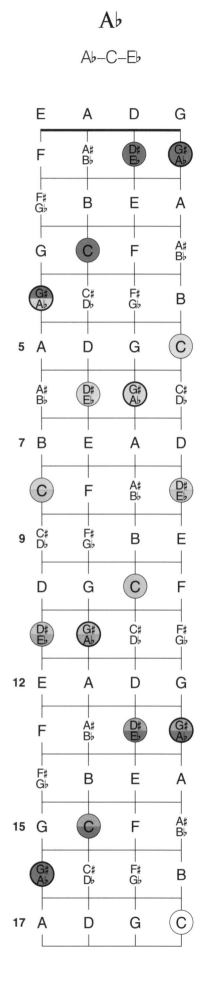

A

A–C#–E

B♭

B♭–D–F

B

B–D#–F#

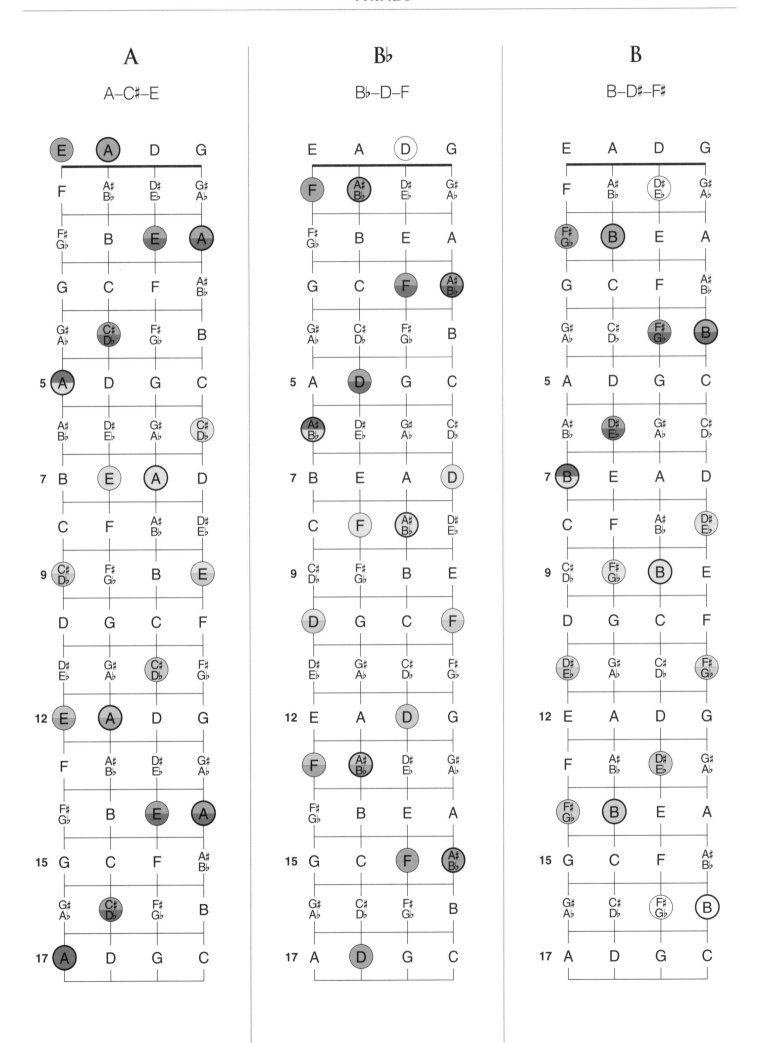

Csus4

C–F–G

C#/D♭sus4

C#–F#–G#/D♭–G♭–A♭

Dsus4

D–G–A

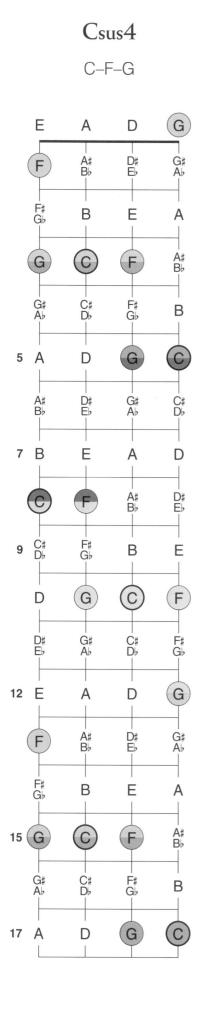

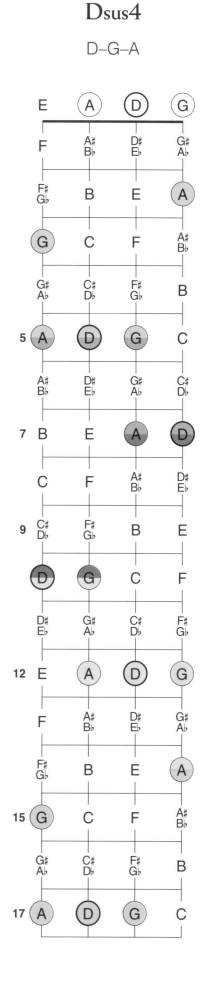

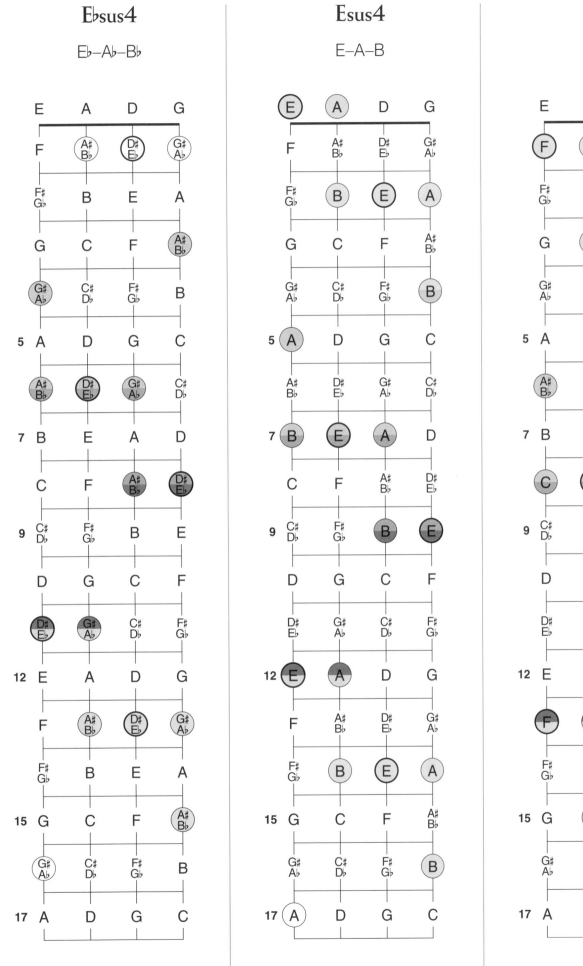

E♭sus4

E♭–A♭–B♭

Esus4

E–A–B

Fsus4

F–B♭–C

F#/G♭sus4

F#–B–C#/G♭–C♭–D♭

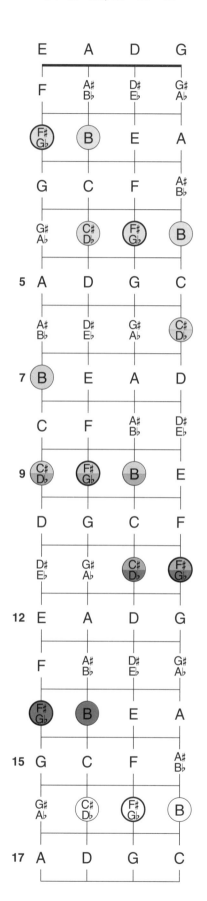

Gsus4

G–C–D

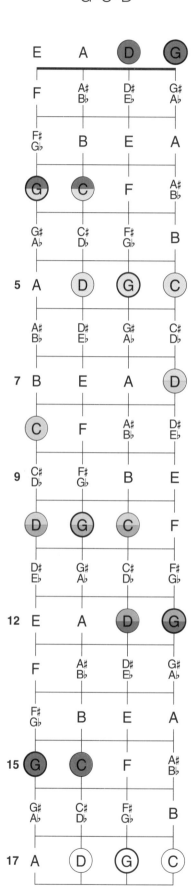

A♭sus4

A♭–D♭–E♭

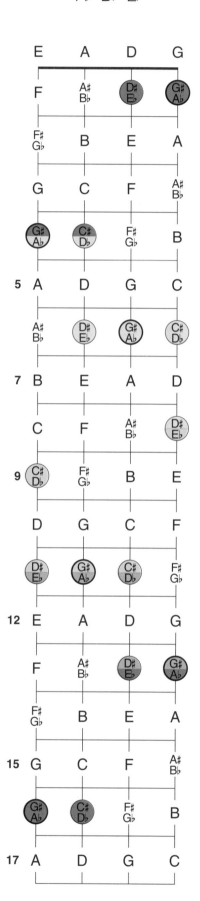

Asus4

A–D–E

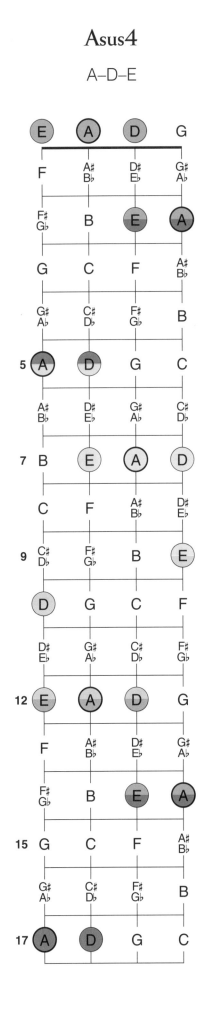

B♭sus4

B♭–E♭–F

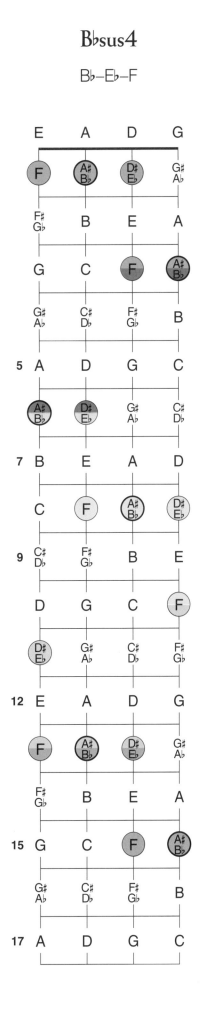

Bsus4

B–E–F♯

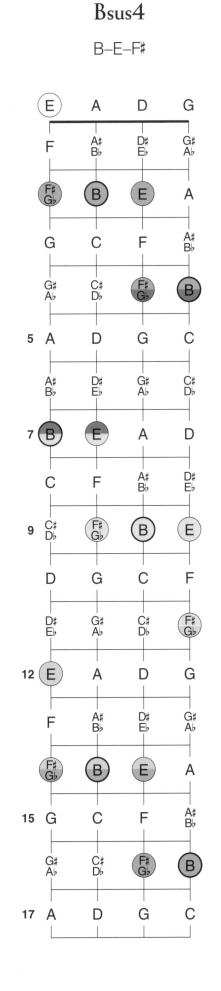

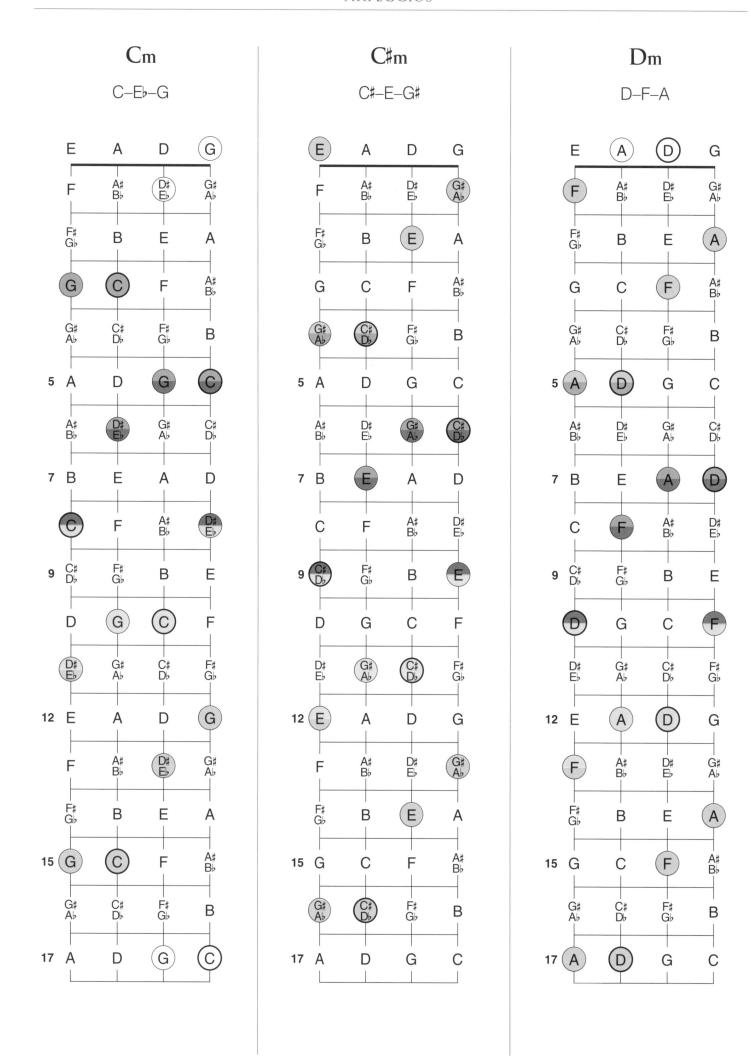

Cm

C–E♭–G

C♯m

C♯–E–G♯

Dm

D–F–A

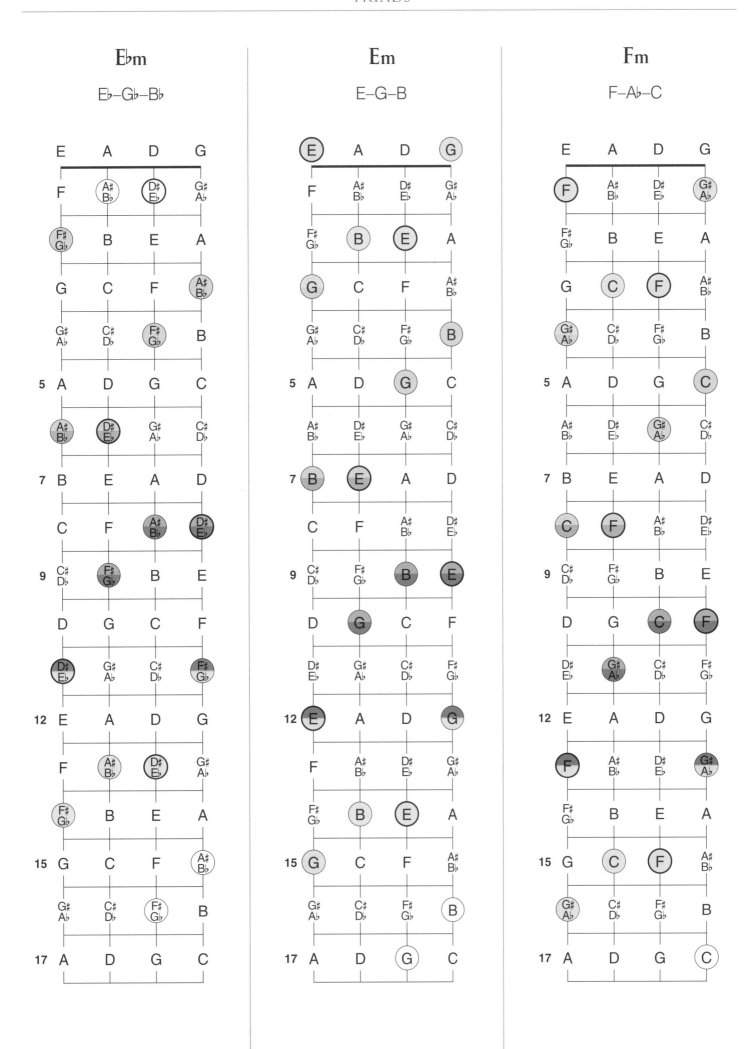

F#m

F#–A–C#

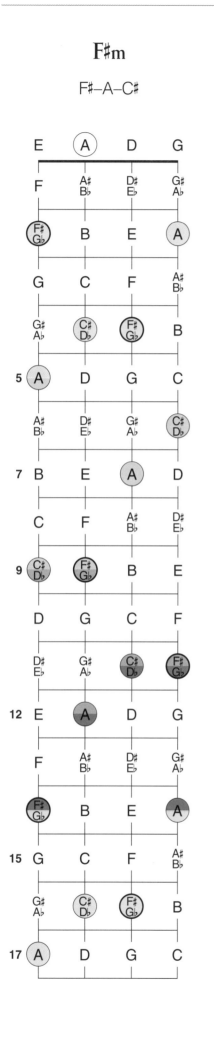

Gm

G–Bb–D

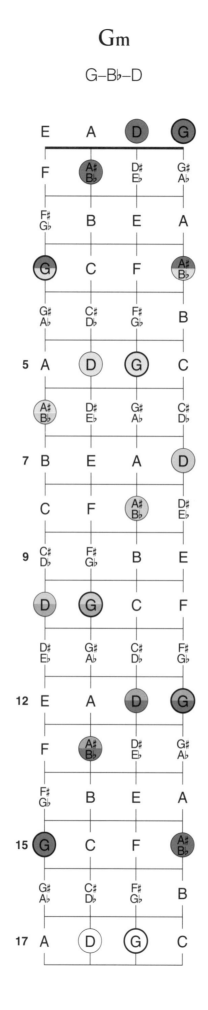

G#/Abm

G#–B–D#/Ab–Cb–Eb

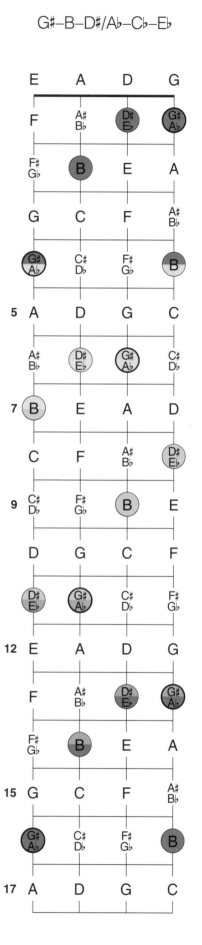

Am
A–C–E

B♭m
B♭–D♭–F

Bm
B–D–F♯

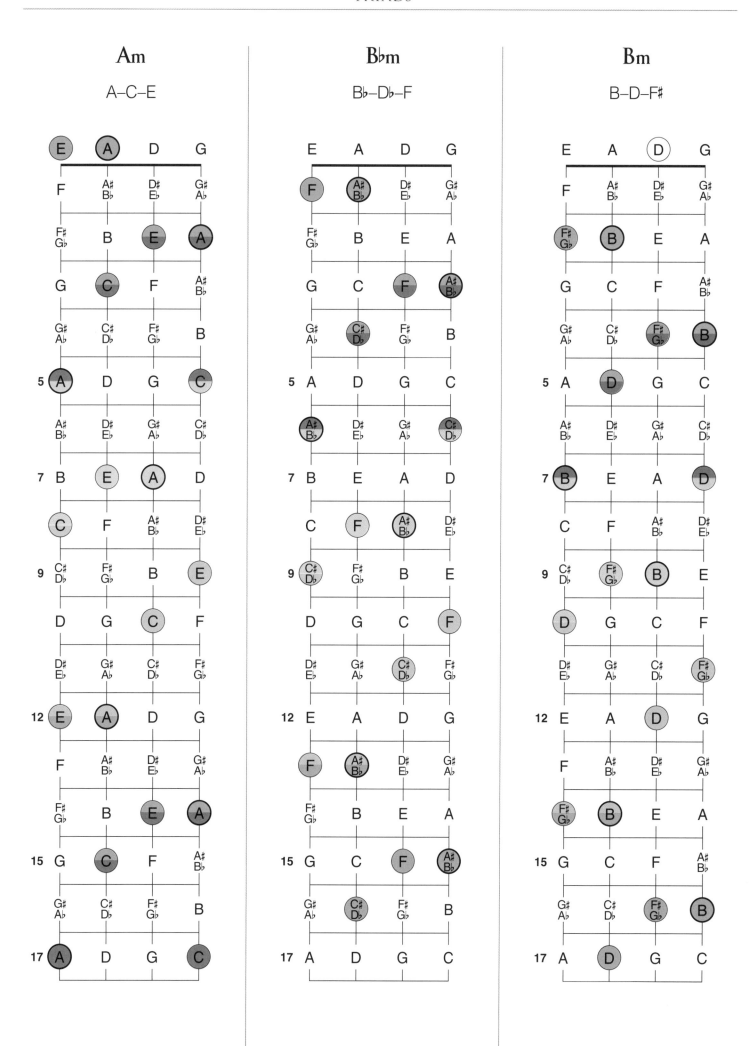

C+

C–E–G#

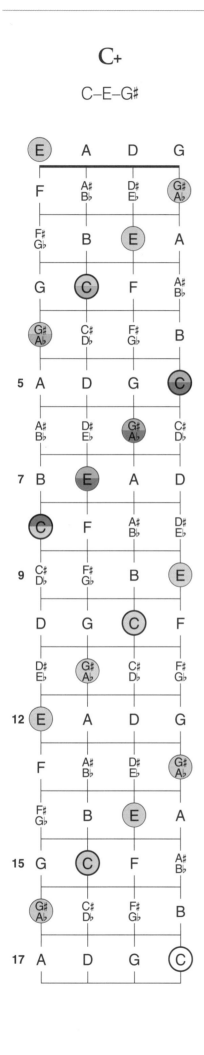

C#/D♭+

C#–E#–G×/D♭–F–A

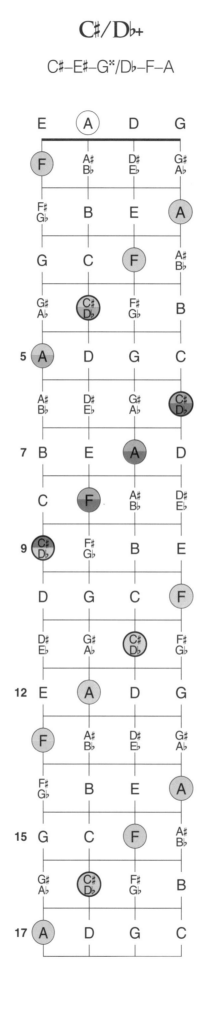

D+

D–F#–A#

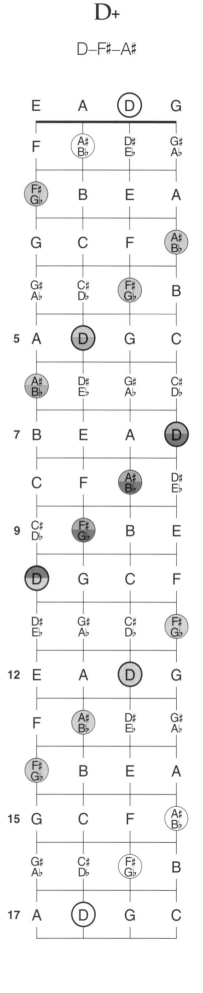

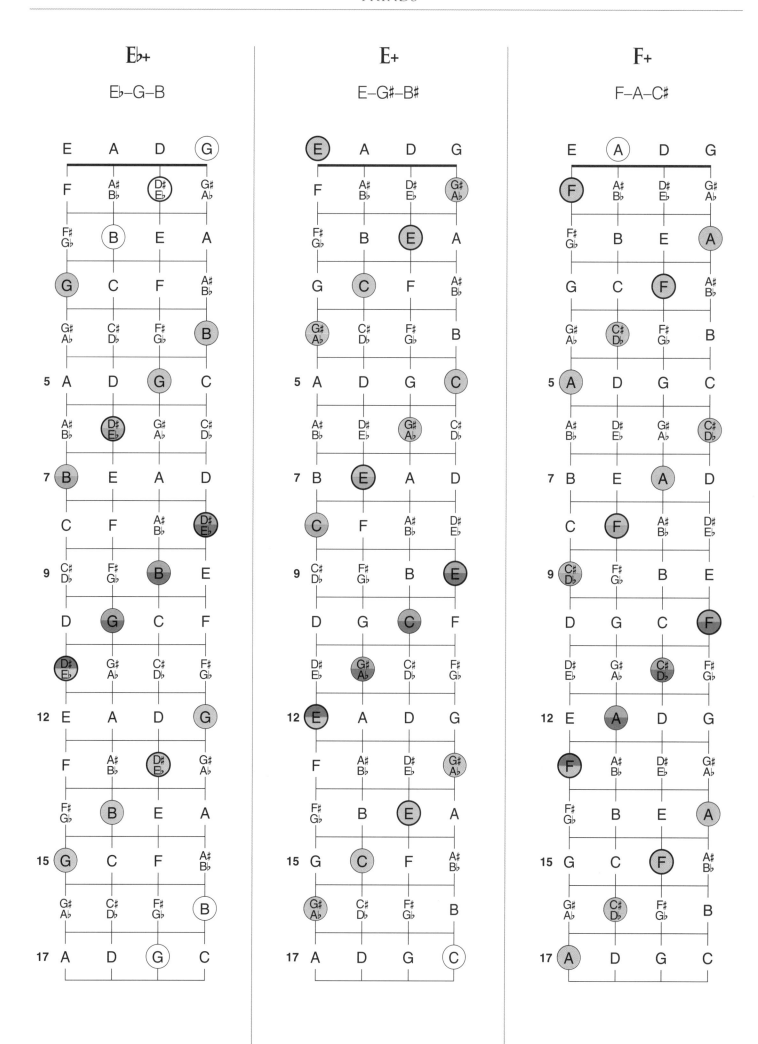

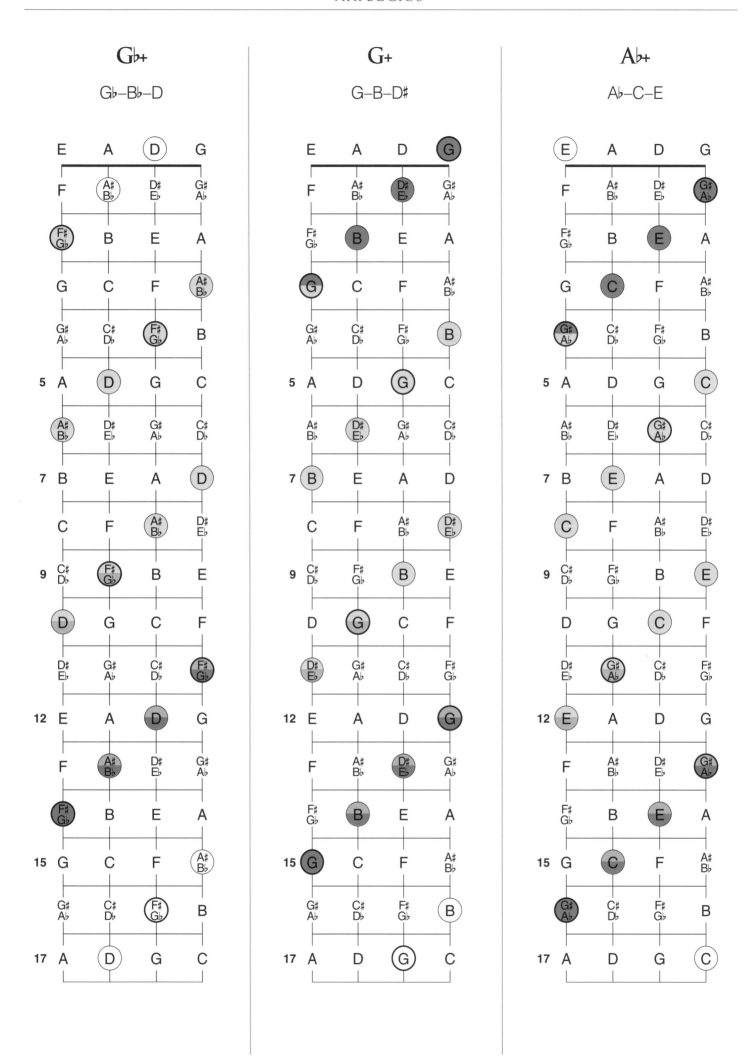

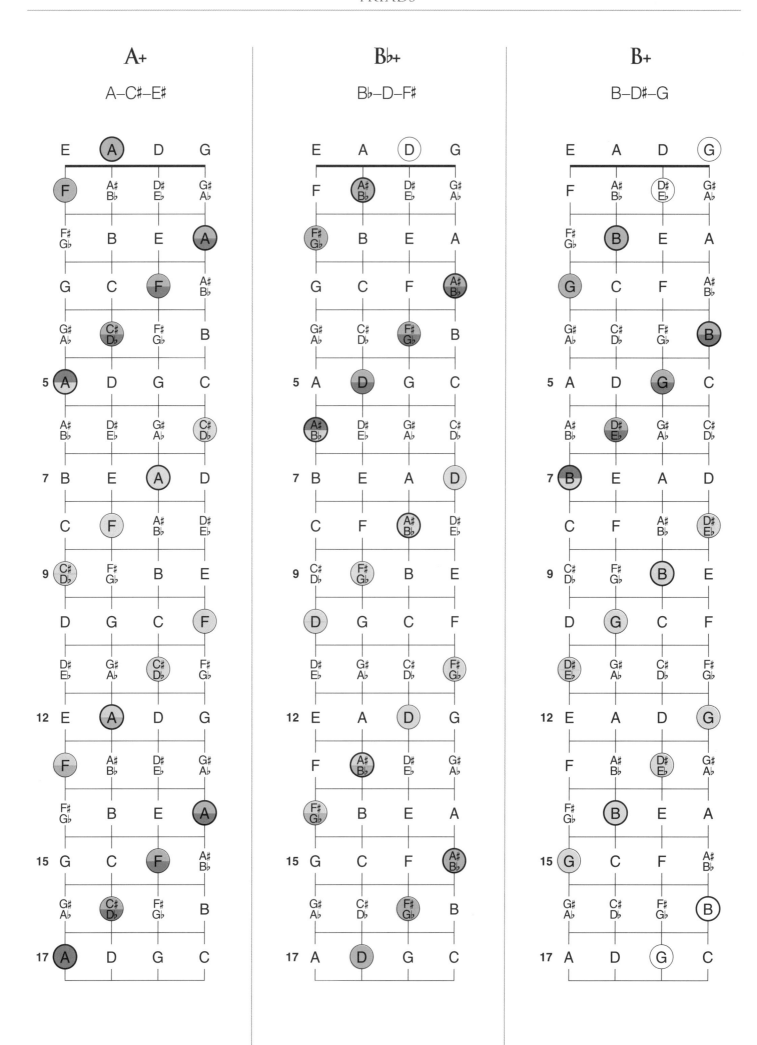

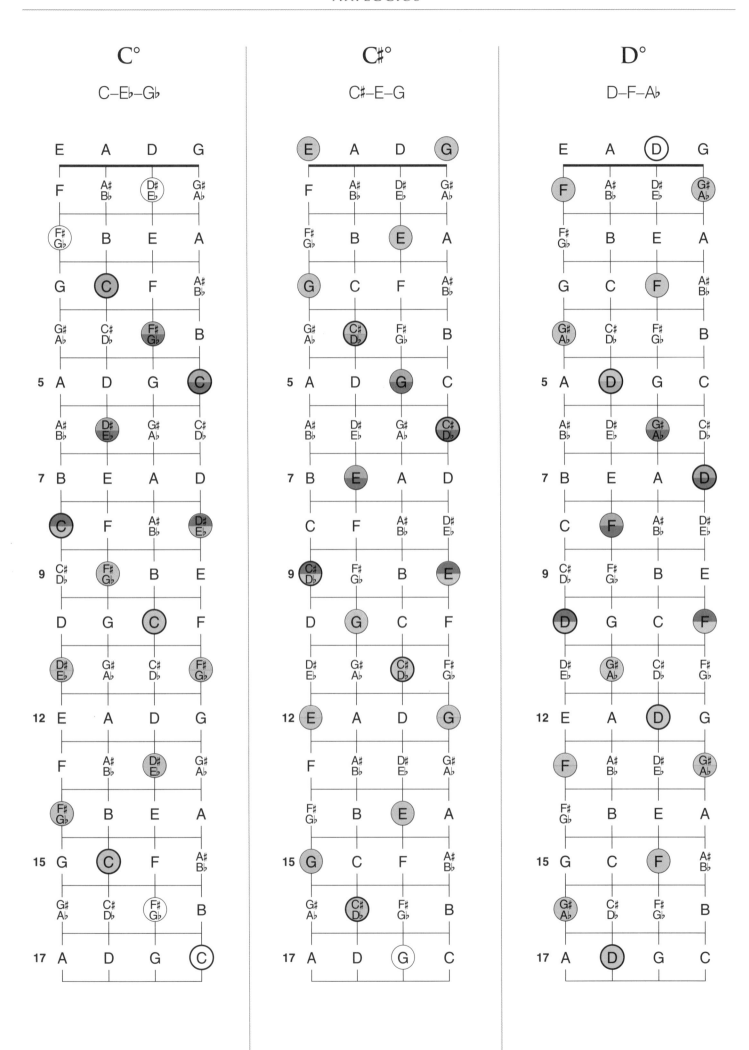

D#°
D#–F#–A

E°
E–G–B♭

F°
F–A♭–C♭

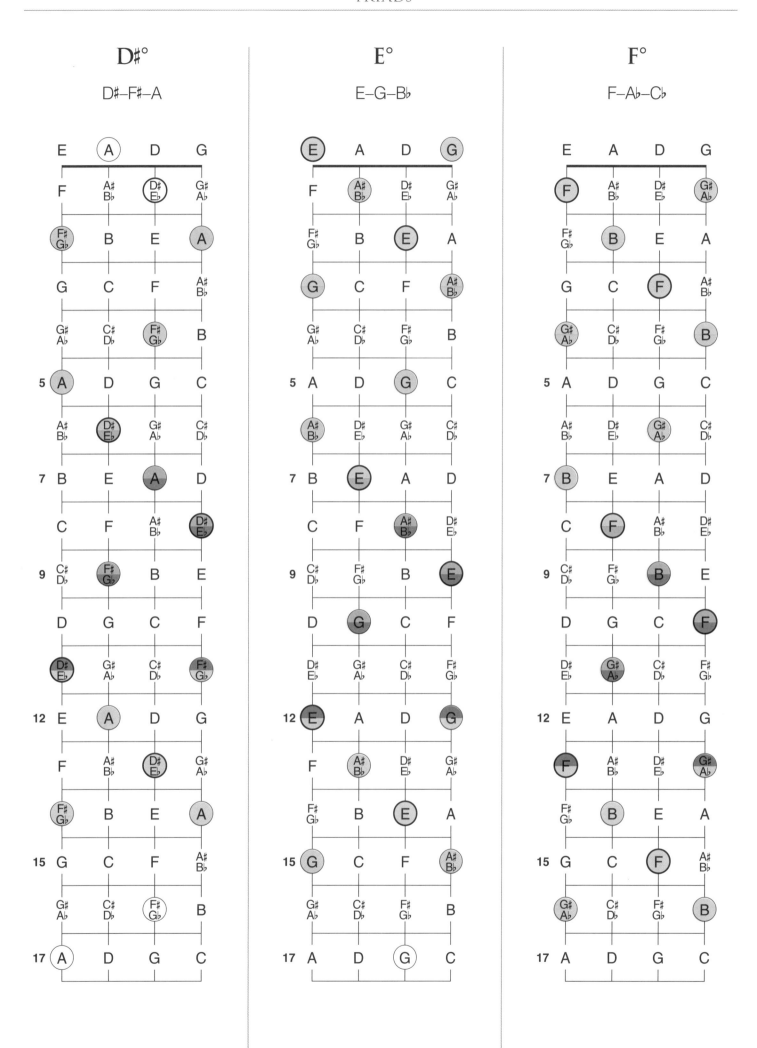

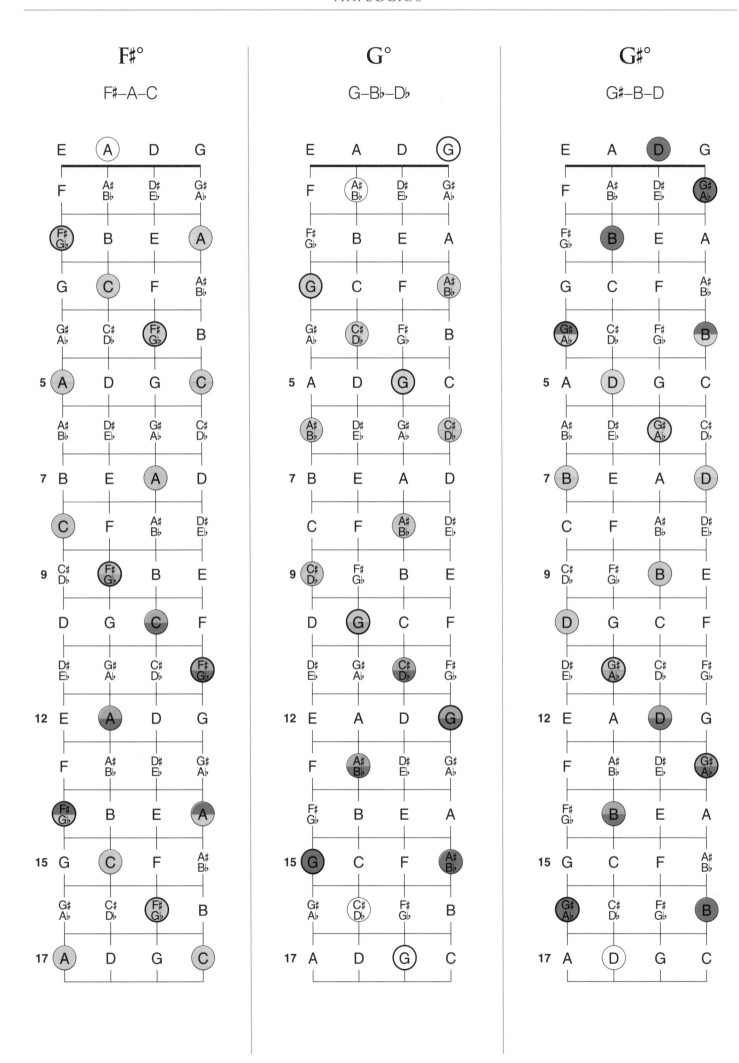

A°

A–C–E♭

B♭°

B♭–D♭–F♭

B°

B–D–F

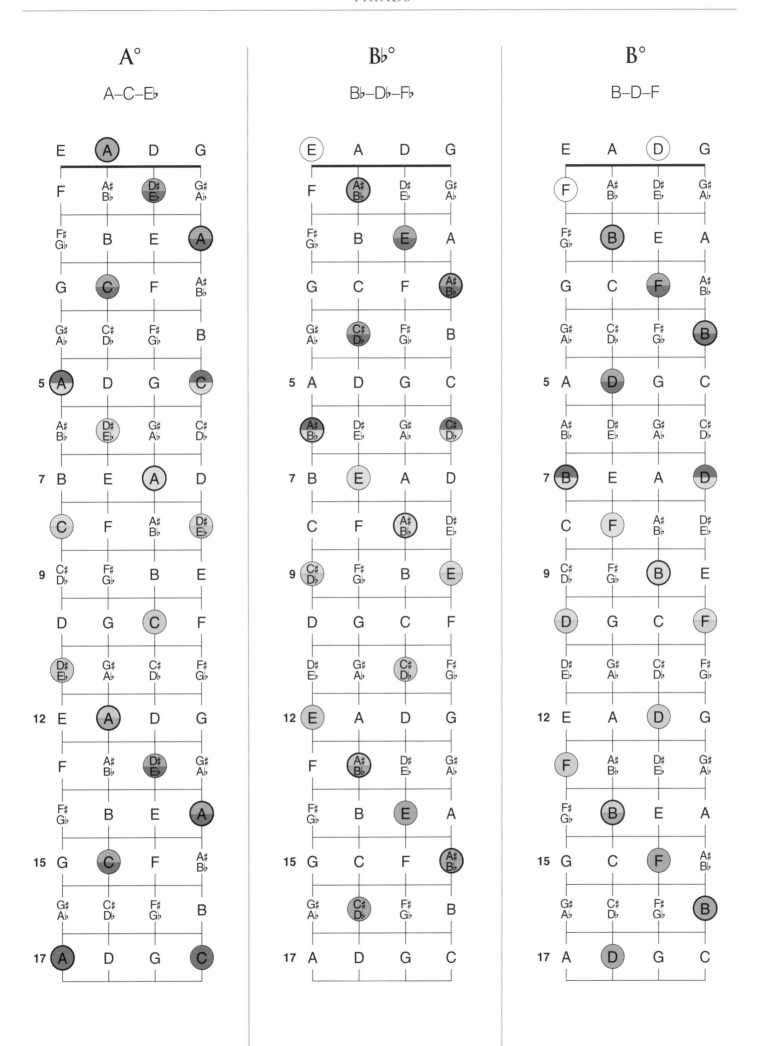

ARPEGGIOS

TRIADS WITH ADDED NOTES

Cadd9

C–E–G–D

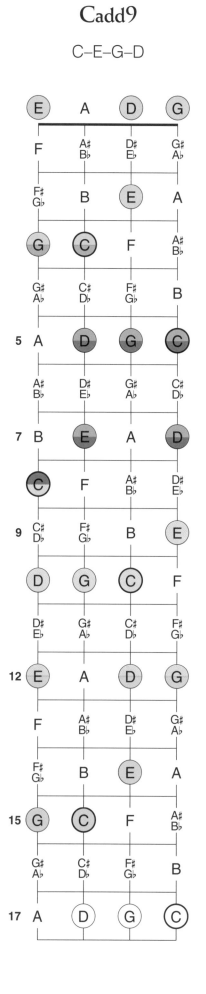

C#/D♭add9

C#–E#–G#–D#/D♭–F–A♭–E♭

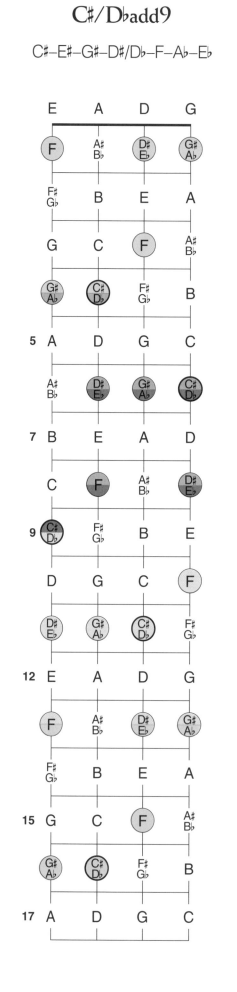

Dadd9

D–F#–A–E

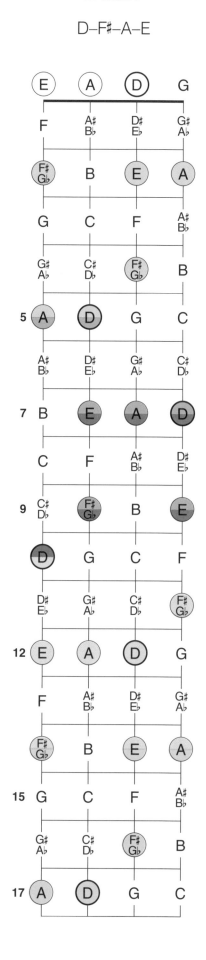

E♭add9

E♭–G–B♭–F

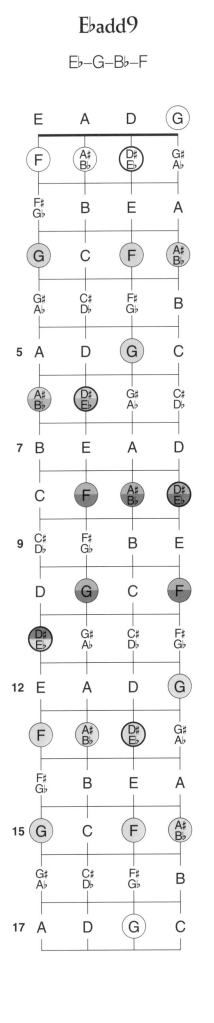

Eadd9

E–G♯–B–F♯

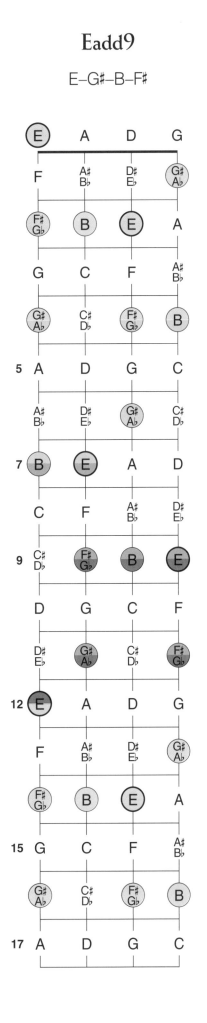

Fadd9

F–A–C–G

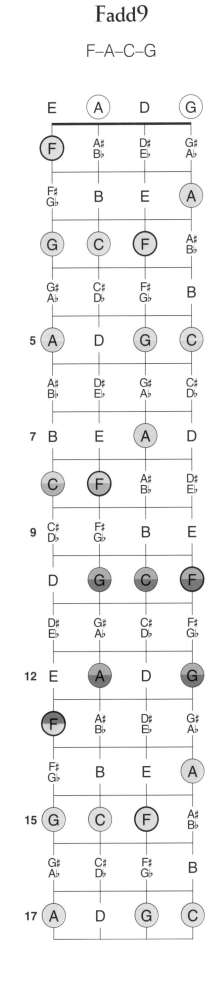

F♯/G♭add9

F♯–A♯–C♯–G♯/G♭–B♭–D♭–A♭

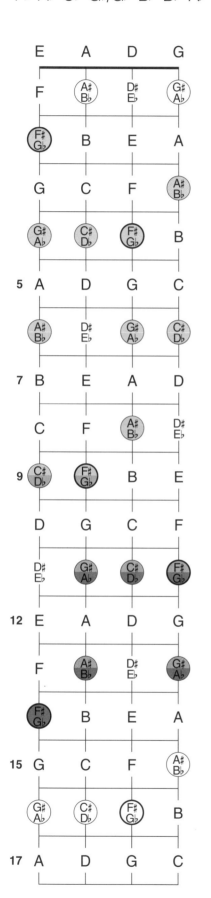

Gadd9

G–B–D–A

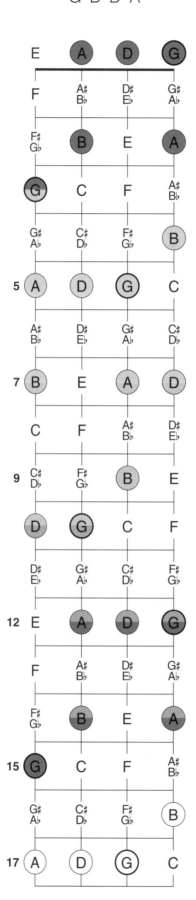

A♭add9

A♭–C–E♭–B♭

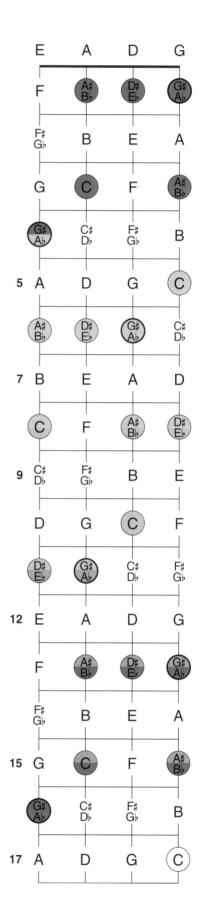

Aadd9

A–C#–E–B

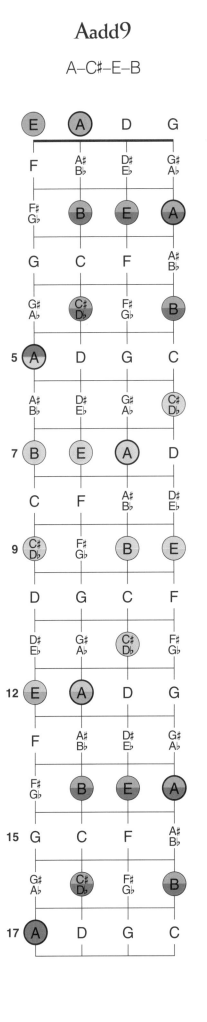

B♭add9

B♭–D–F–C

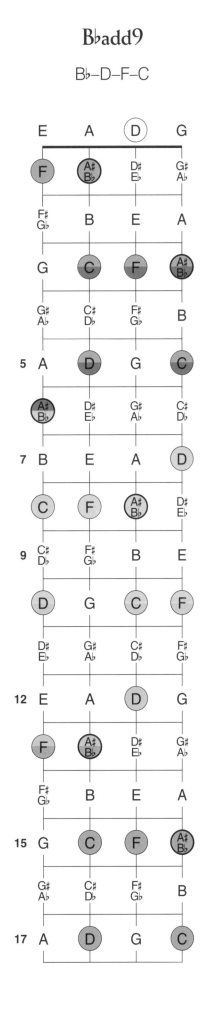

Badd9

B–D#–F#–C#

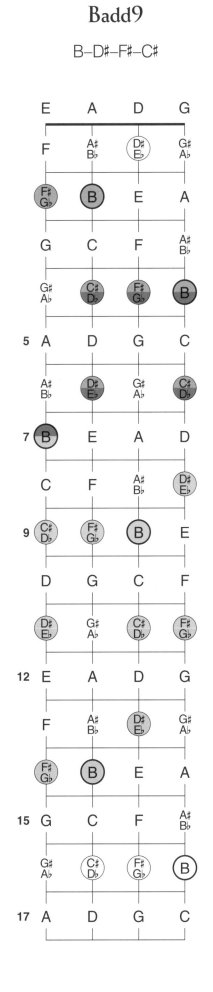

Cm(add9)

C–E♭–G–D

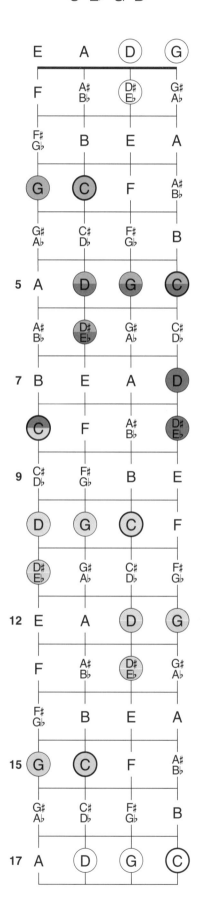

C♯m(add9)

C♯–E–G♯–D♯

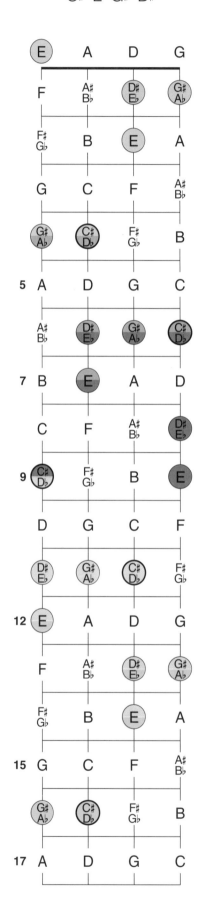

Dm(add9)

D–F–A–E

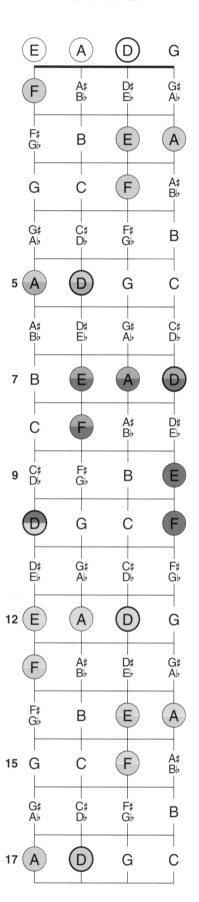

E♭m(add9)

E♭–G♭–B♭–F

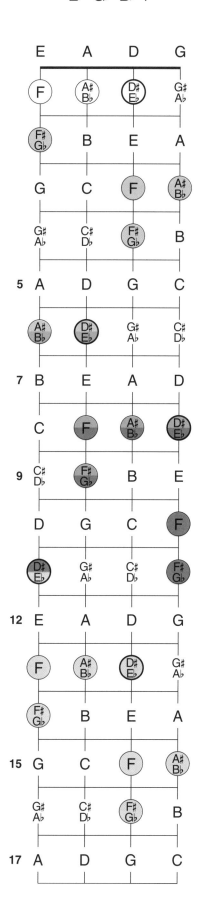

Em(add9)

E–G–B–F♯

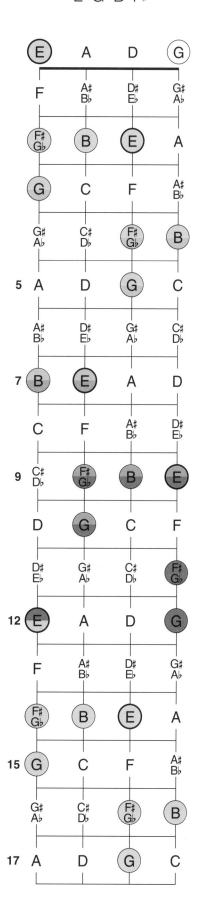

Fm(add9)

F–A♭–C–G

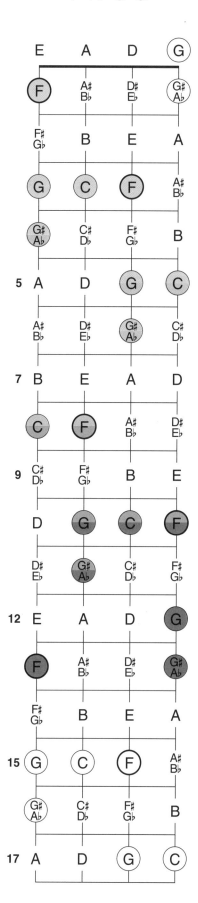

F#m(add9)

F#–A–C#–G#

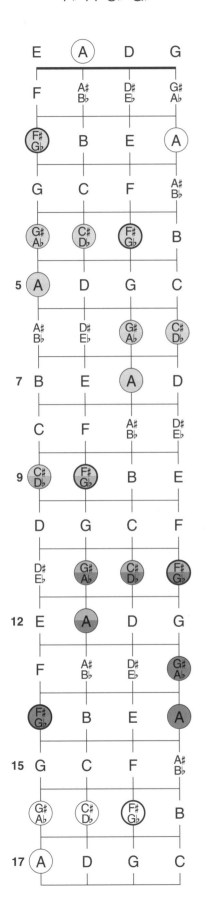

Gm(add9)

G–Bb–D–A

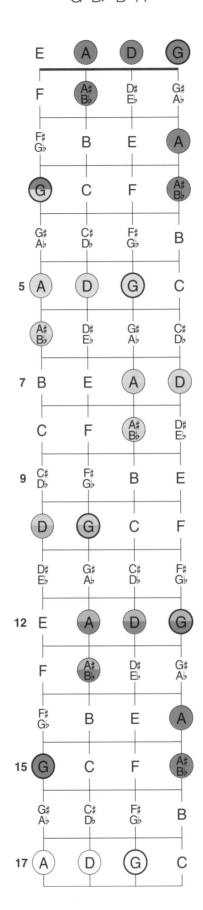

Abm(add9)

Ab–Cb–Eb–Bb

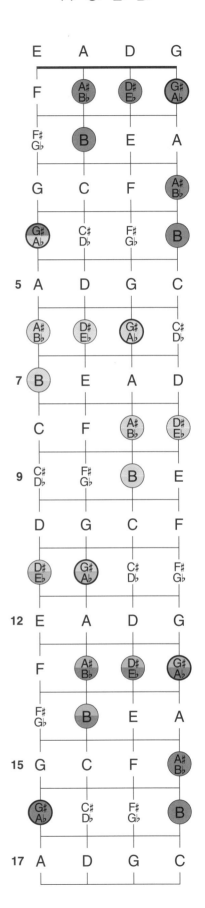

Am(add9)

A–C–E–B

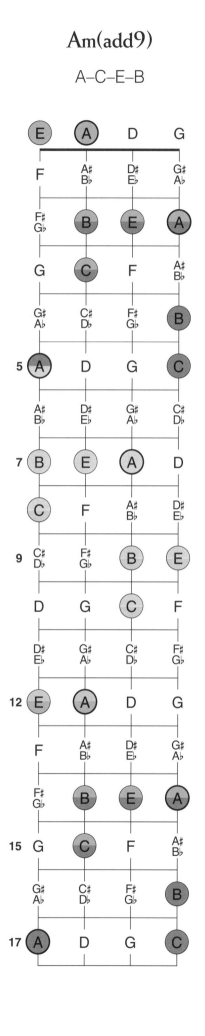

B♭m(add9)

B♭–D♭–F–C

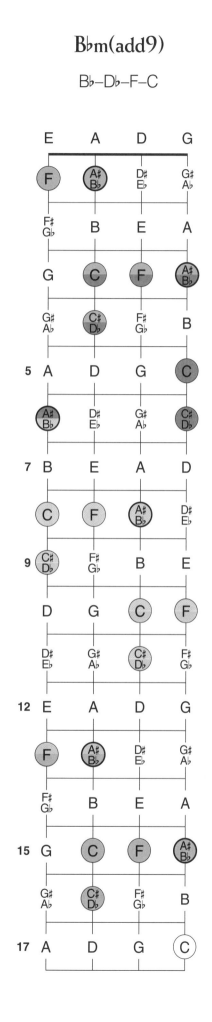

Bm(add9)

B–D–F♯–C♯

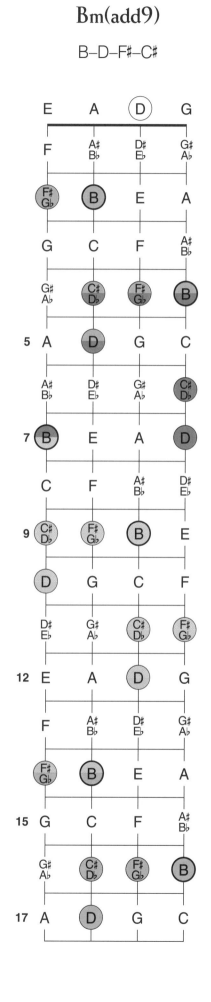

C6

C–E–G–A

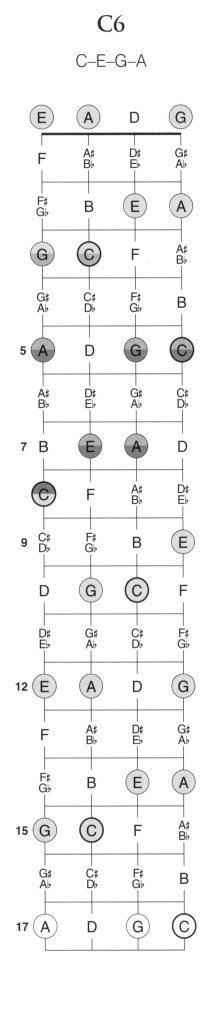

C#/D♭6

C#–E#–G#–A#/D♭–F–A♭–B♭

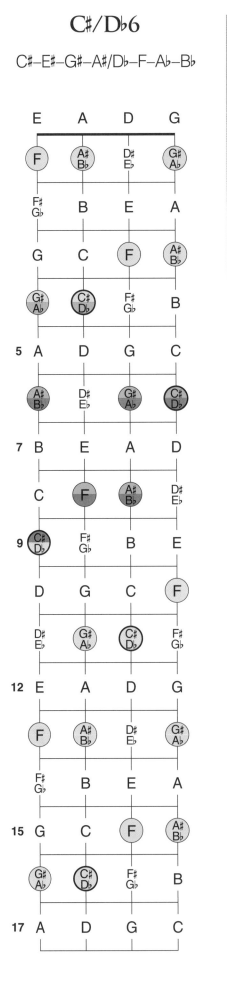

D6

D–F#–A–B

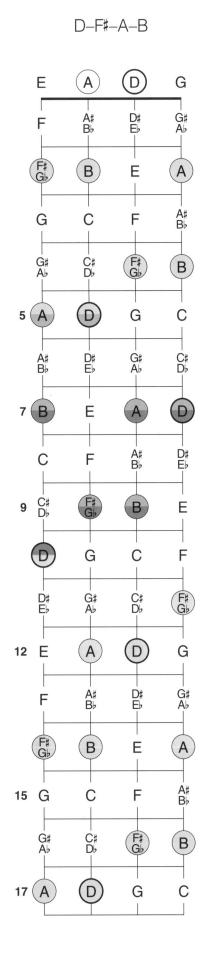

E♭6

Eb–G–Bb–C

E6

E–G#–B–C#

F6

F–A–C–D

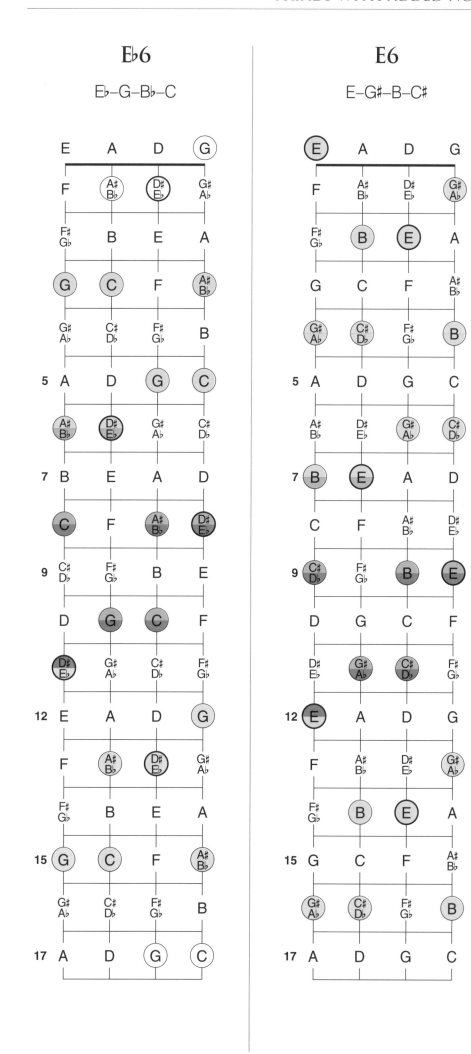

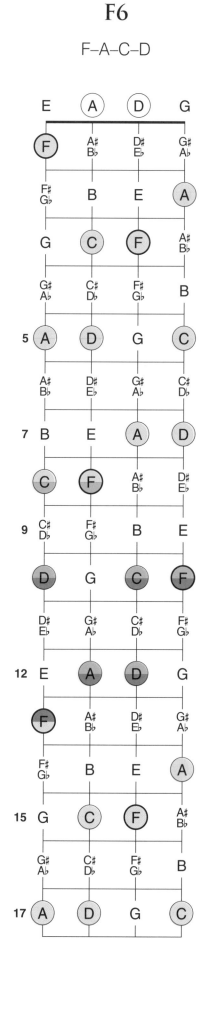

F#/G♭6

F#–A#–C#–D#/G♭–B♭–D♭–E♭

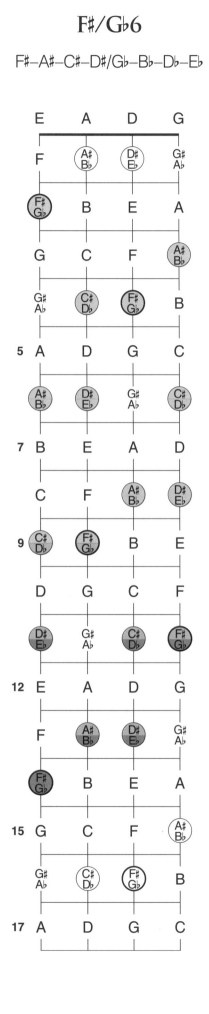

G6

G–B–D–E

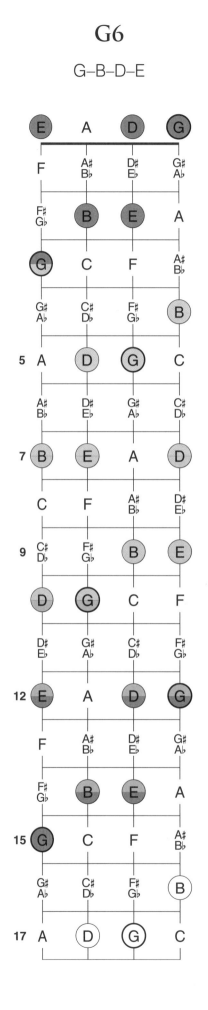

A♭6

A♭–C–E♭–F

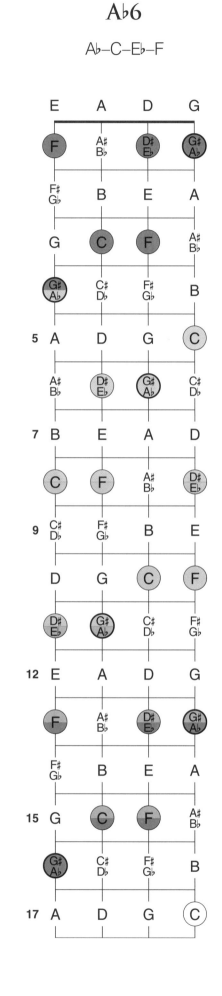

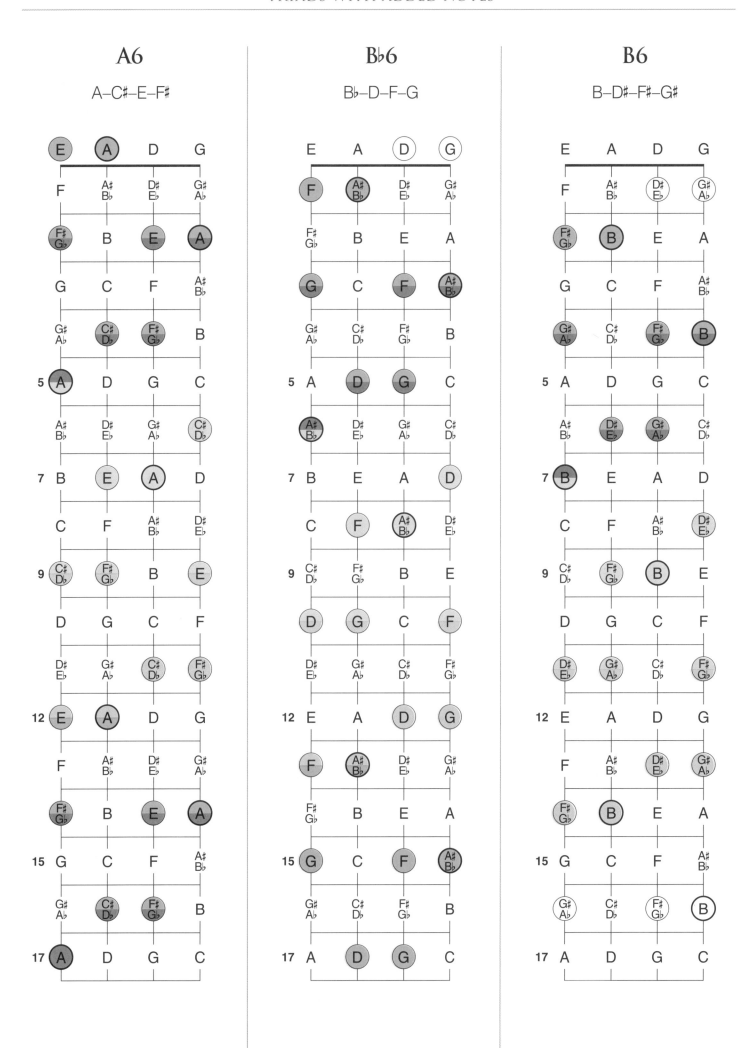

Cm6

C–E♭–G–A

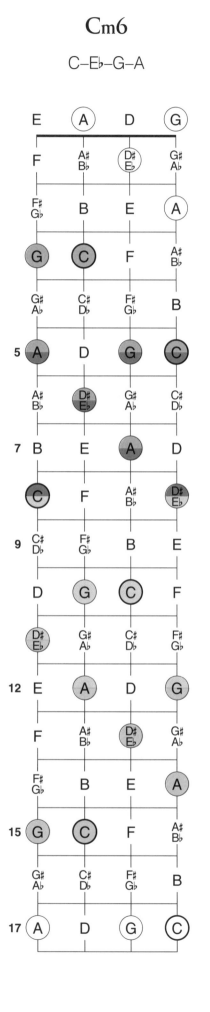

C#m6

C#–E–G#–A#

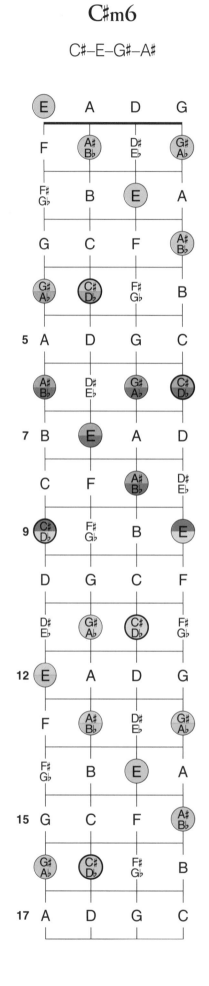

Dm6

D–F–A–B

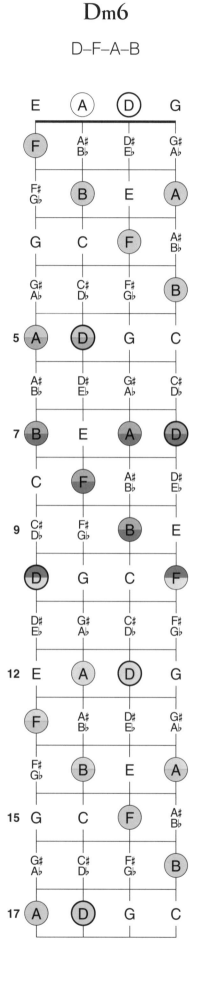

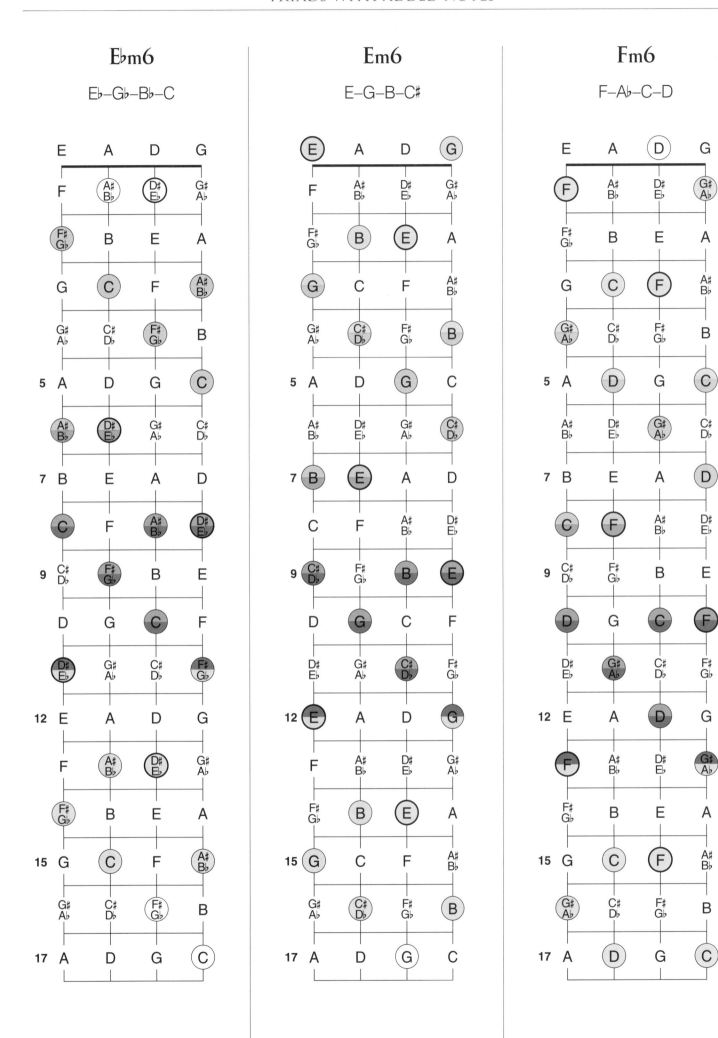

F#m6

F#–A–C#–D#

Gm6

G–B♭–D–E

A♭m6

A♭–C♭–E♭–F

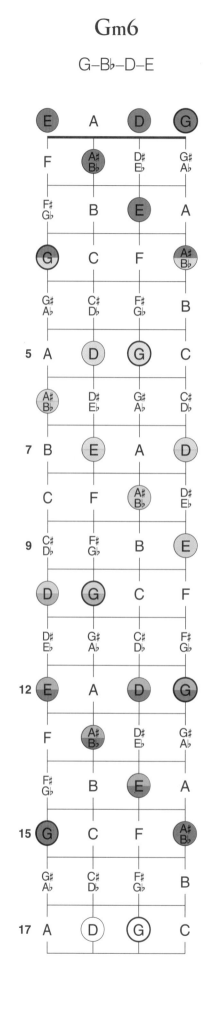

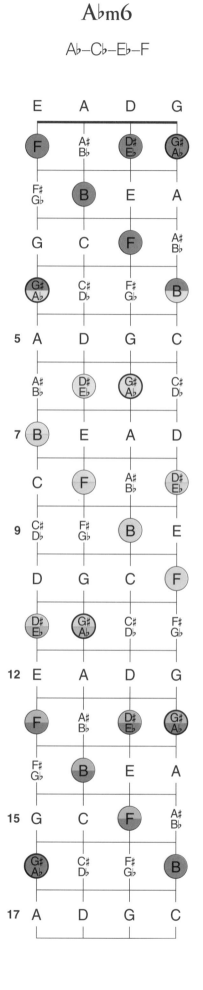

Am6

A–C–E–F#

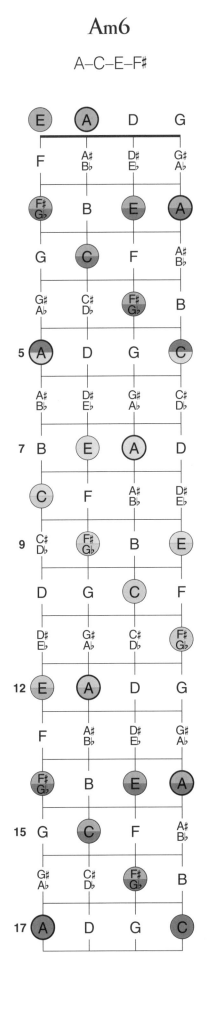

B♭m6

B♭–D♭–F–G

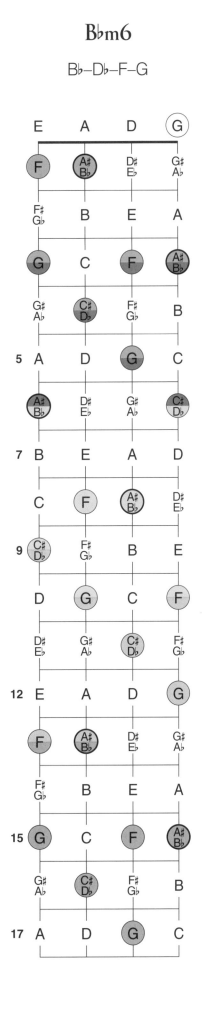

Bm6

B–D–F#–G#

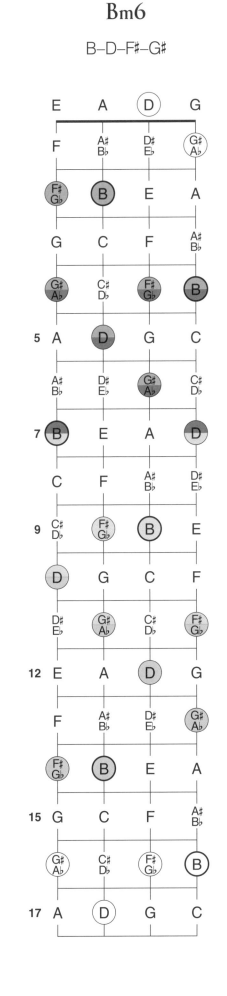

C⁶₉

C–E–G–A–D

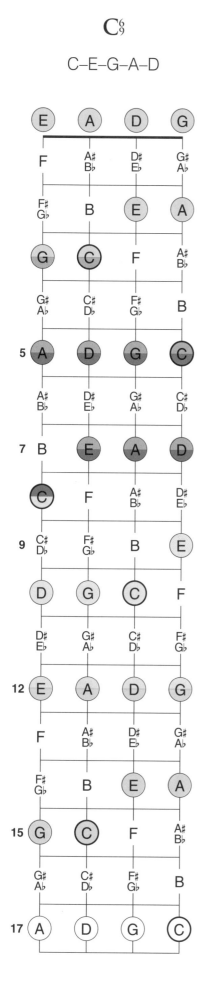

C♯/D♭⁶₉

C♯–E♯–G♯–A♯–D♯/D♭–F–A♭–B♭–E♭

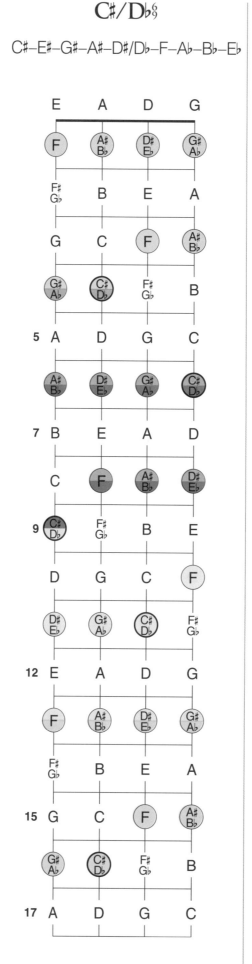

D⁶₉

D–F♯–A–B–E

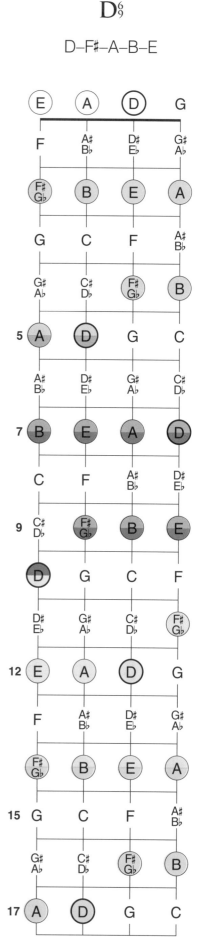

$E\flat^6_9$

Eb–G–Bb–C–F

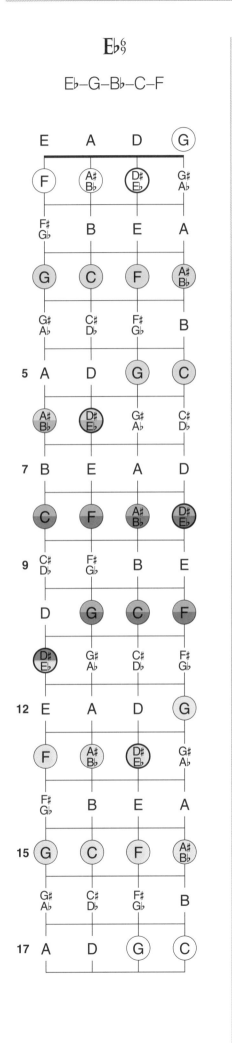

E^6_9

E–G#–B–C#–F#

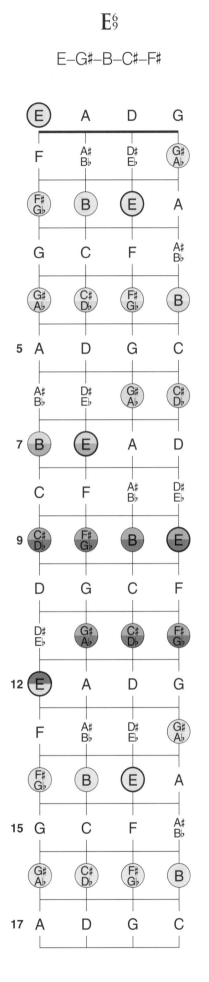

F^6_9

F–A–C–D–G

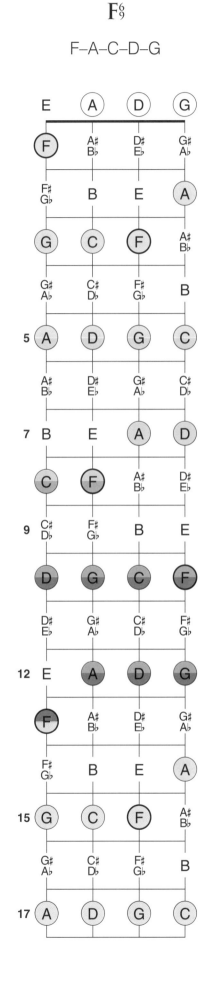

F#/G♭$^6_9$

F#–A#–C#–D#–G#/G♭–B♭–D♭–E♭–A♭

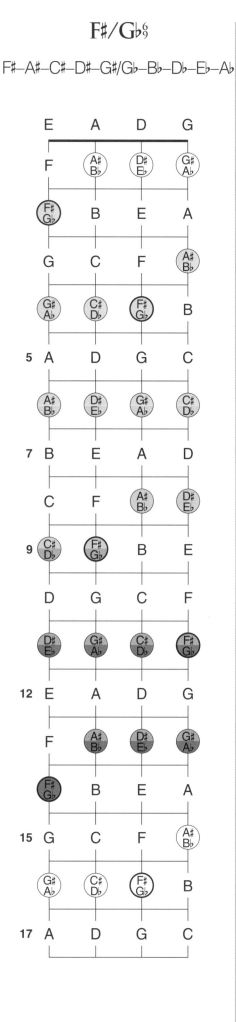

G$^6_9$

G–B–D–E–A

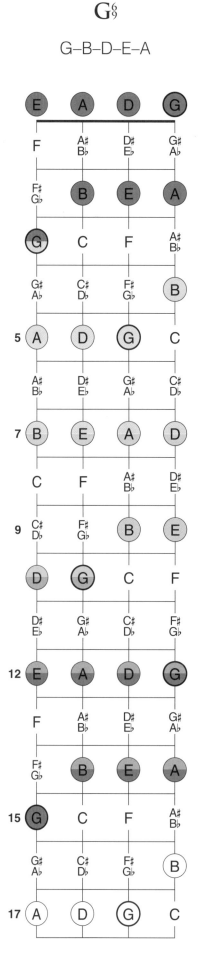

A♭$^6_9$

A♭–C–E♭–F–B♭

A$^6_9$

A–C#–E–F#–B

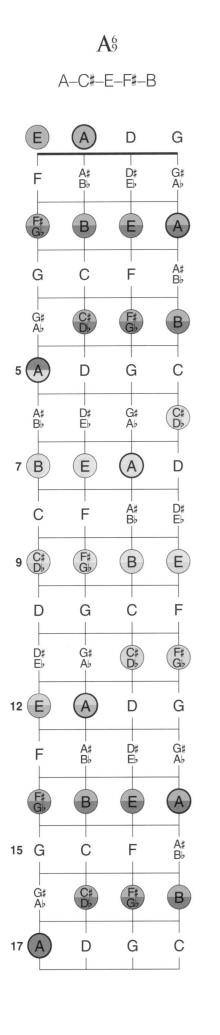

B♭$^6_9$

B♭–D–F–G–C

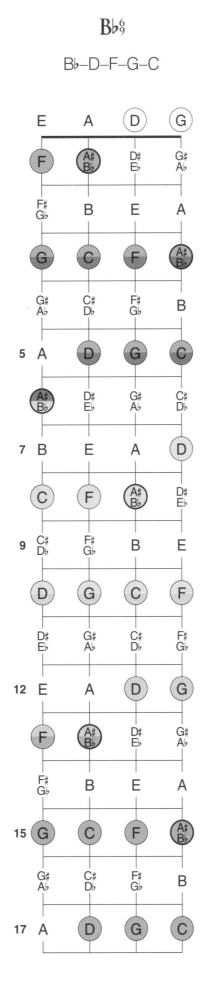

B$^6_9$

B–D#–F#–G#–C#

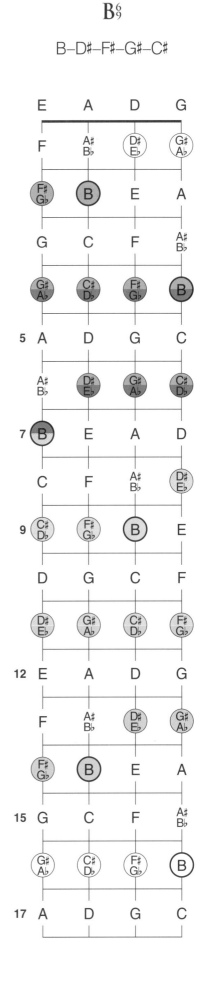

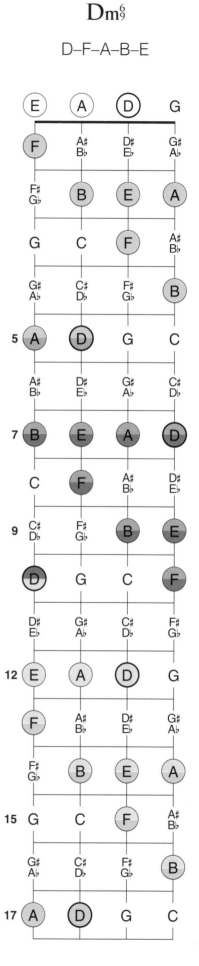

Cm$^6_9$

C–E♭–G–A–D

C♯m$^6_9$

C♯–E–G♯–A♯–D♯

Dm$^6_9$

D–F–A–B–E

E♭m$^6_9$

E♭–G♭–B♭–C–F

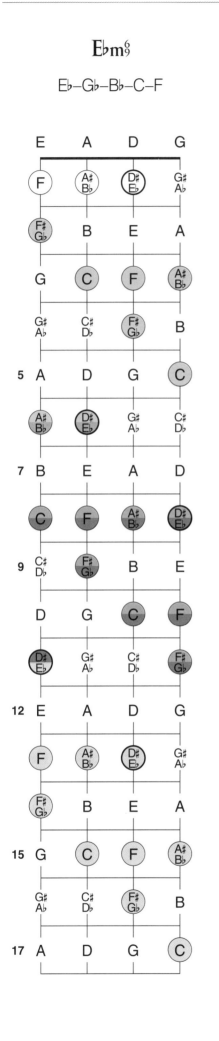

Em$^6_9$

E–G–B–C♯–F♯

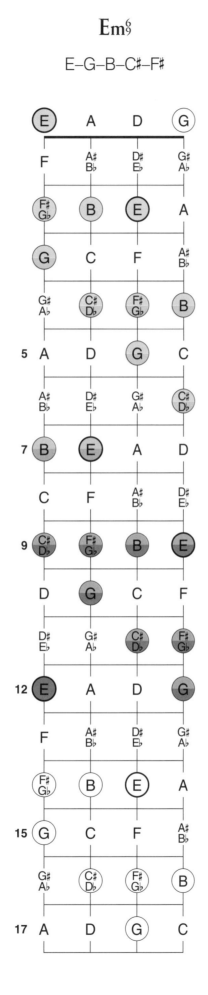

Fm$^6_9$

F–A♭–C–D–G

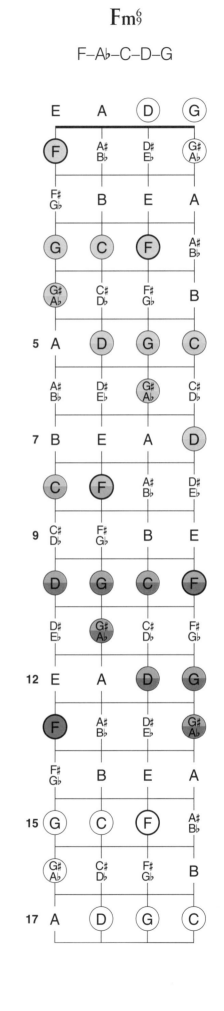

F#m⁶₉

F#–A–C#–D#–G#

Gm⁶₉

G–B♭–D–E–A

A♭m⁶₉

A♭–C♭–E♭–F–B♭

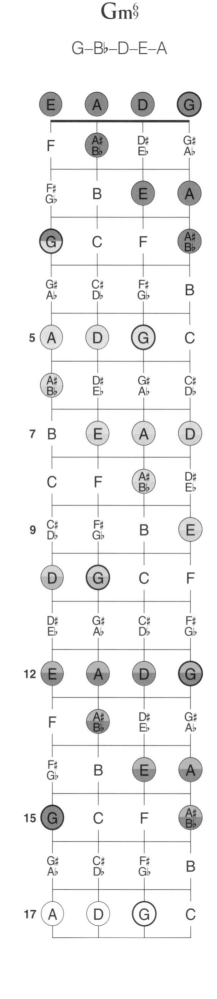

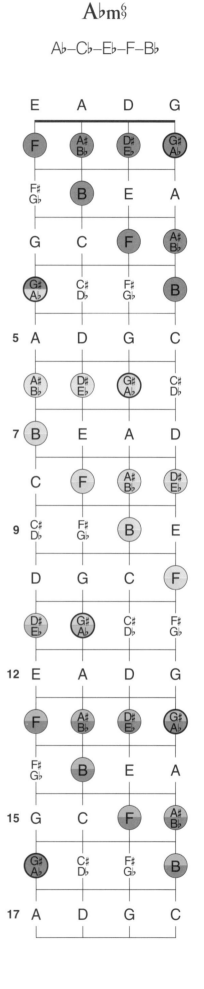

Am⁶₉

A–C–E–F#–B

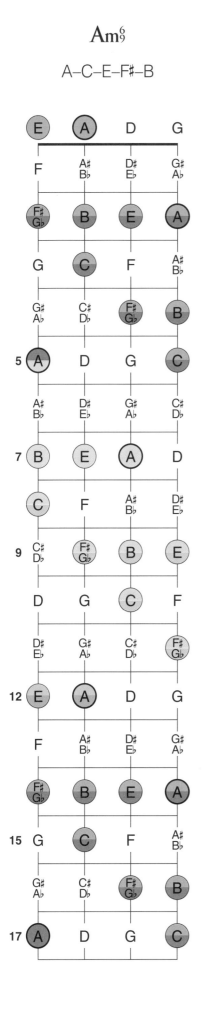

B♭m⁶₉

B♭–D♭–F–G–C

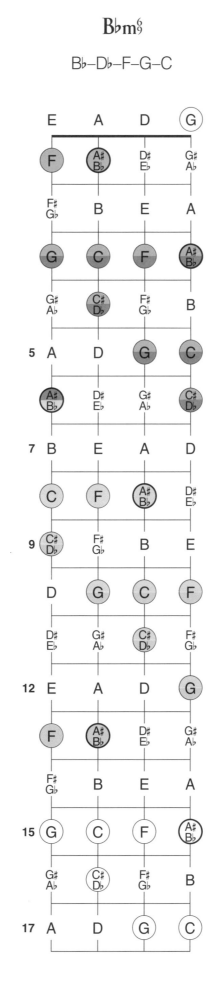

Bm⁶₉

B–D–F#–G#–C#

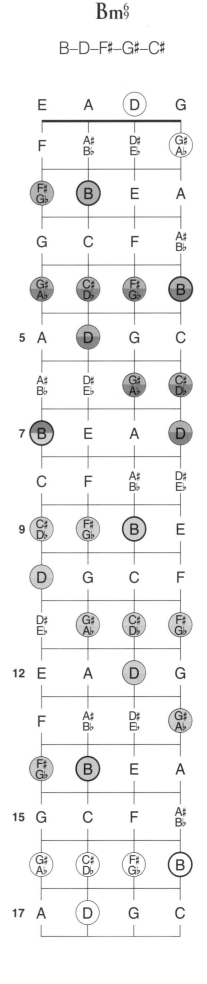

ARPEGGIOS

SEVENTH CHORDS

Cmaj7
C–E–G–B

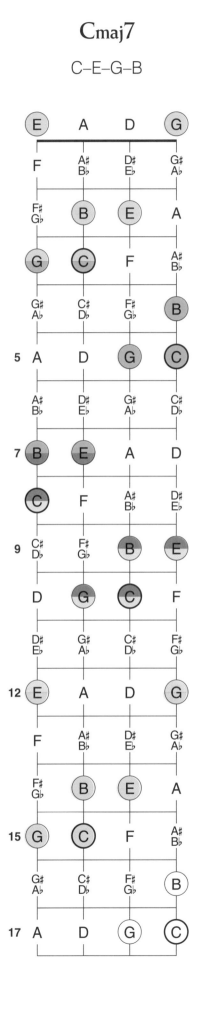

C#/D♭maj7
C#–E#–G#–B#/D♭–F–A♭–C

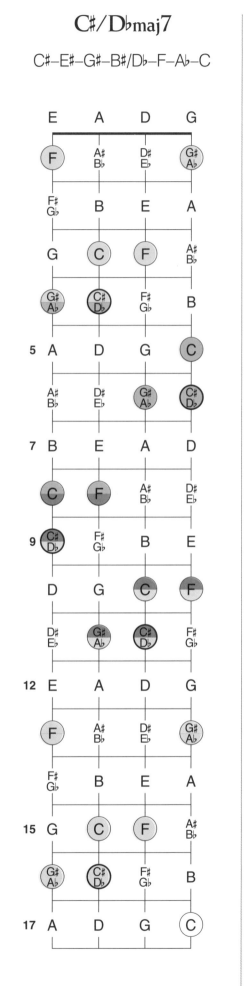

Dmaj7
D–F#–A–C#

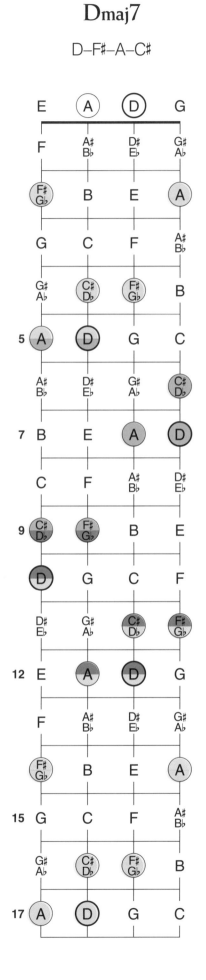

E♭maj7

E♭–G–B♭–D

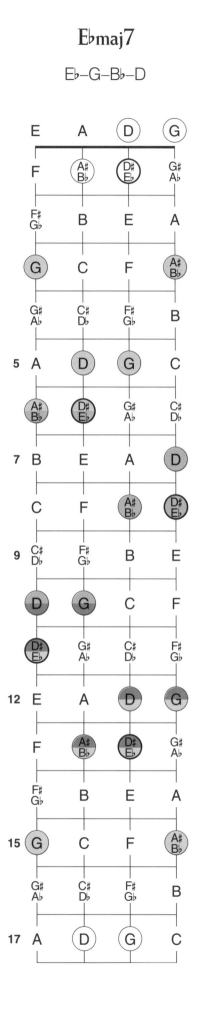

Emaj7

E–G#–B–D#

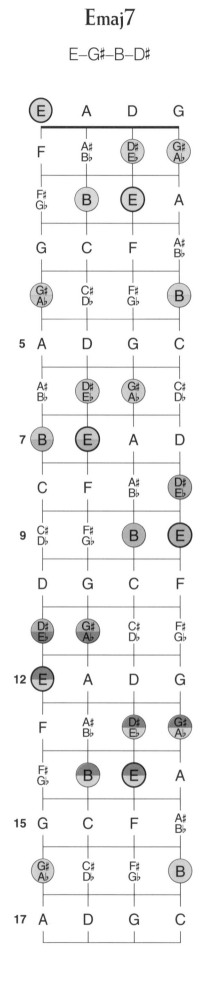

Fmaj7

F–A–C–E

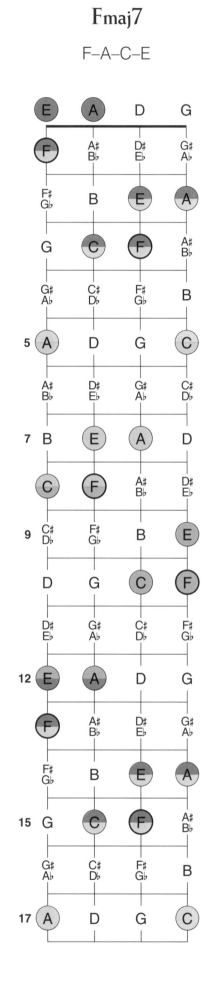

F♯/G♭maj7

F♯–A♯–C♯–E♯/G♭–B♭–D♭–F

Gmaj7

G–B–D–F♯

A♭maj7

A♭–C–E♭–G

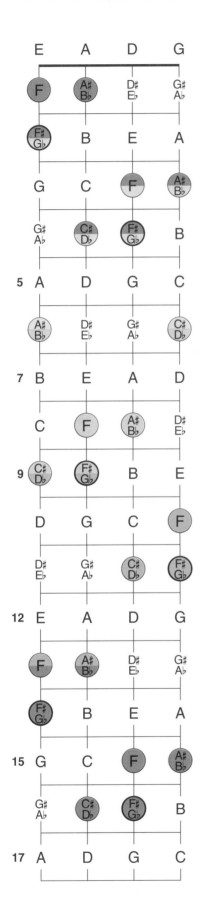
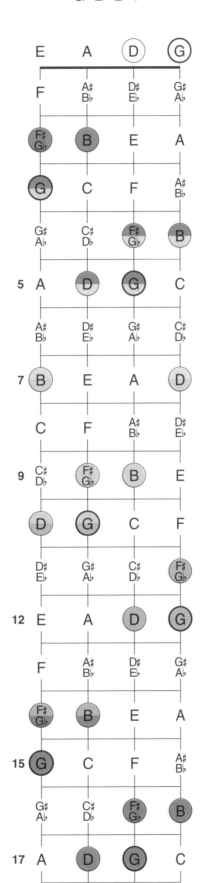
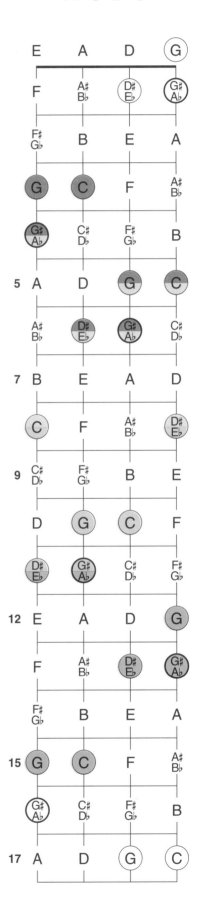

Amaj7

A–C#–E–G#

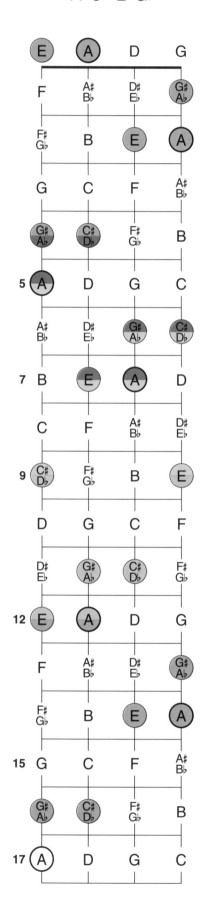

B♭maj7

B♭–D–F–A

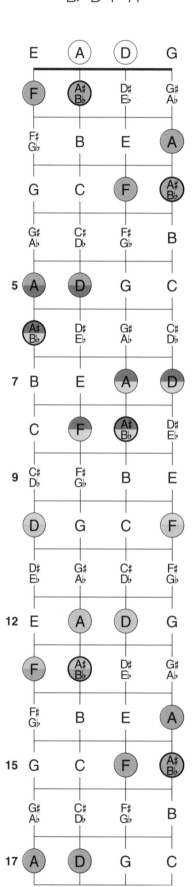

Bmaj7

B–D#–F#–A#

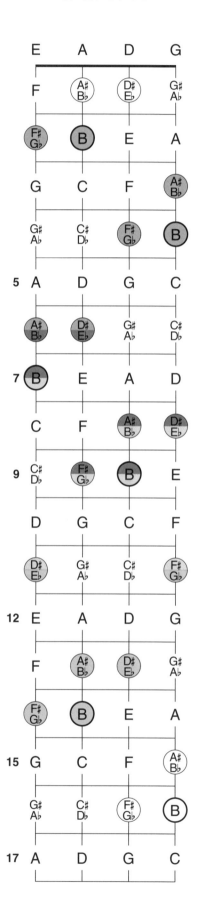

C7

C–E–G–B♭

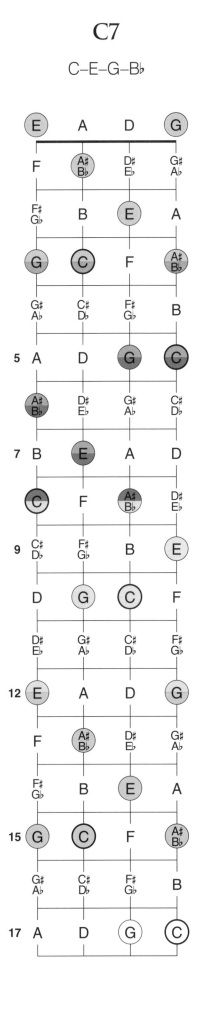

C♯/D♭7

C♯–E♯–G♯–B/D♭–F–A♭–C♭

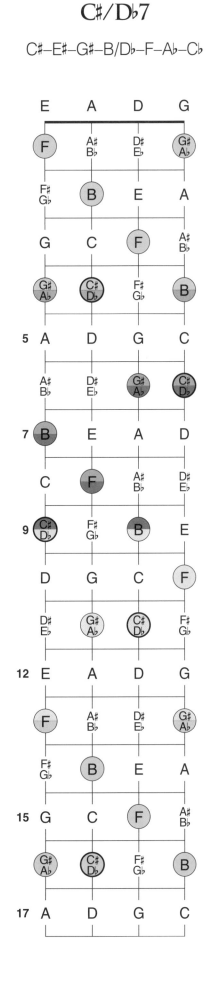

D7

D–F♯–A–C

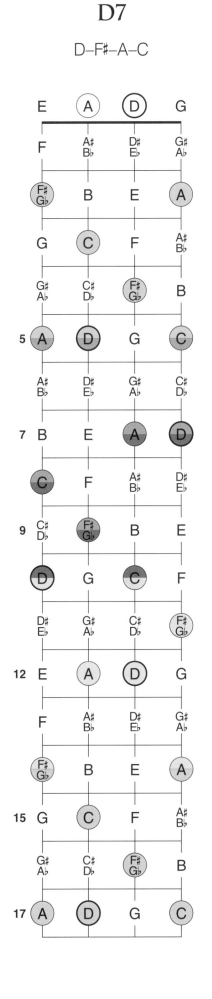

E♭7

E♭–G–B♭–D♭

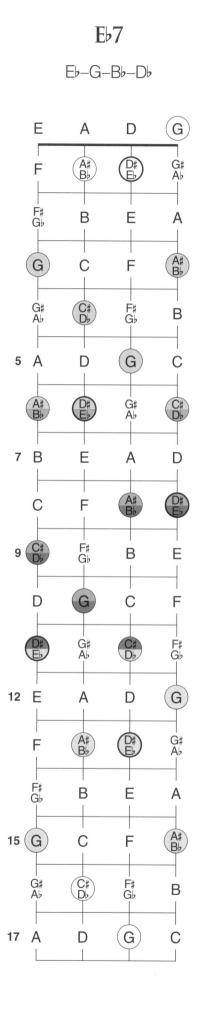

E7

E–G#–B–D

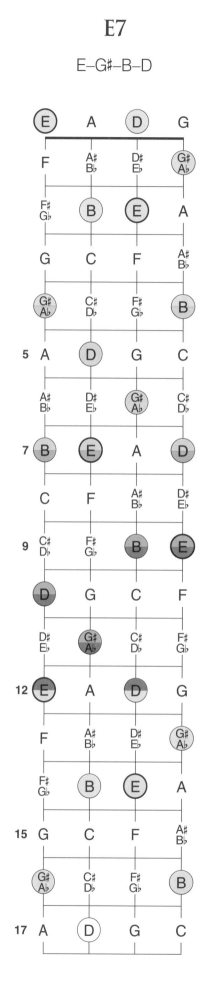

F7

F–A–C–E♭

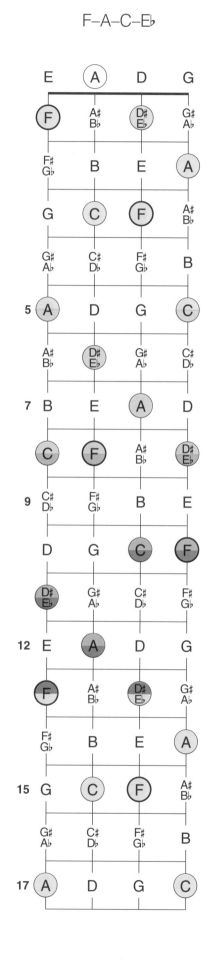

F#/G♭7

F#–A#–C#–E/G♭–B♭–D♭–F♭

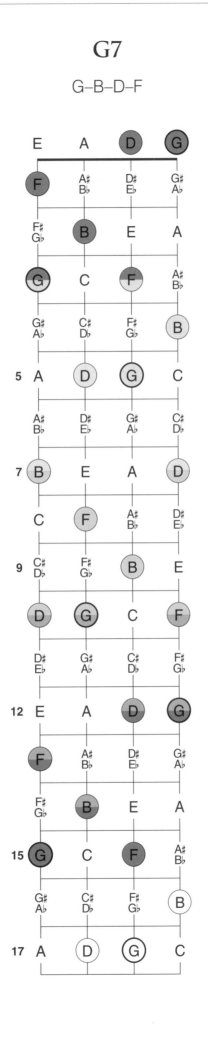

G7

G–B–D–F

A♭7

A♭–C–E♭–G♭

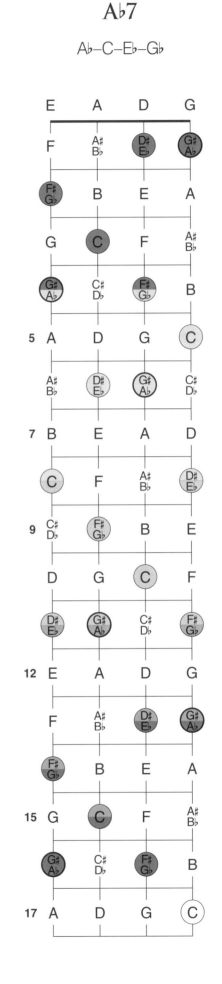

A7

A–C#–E–G

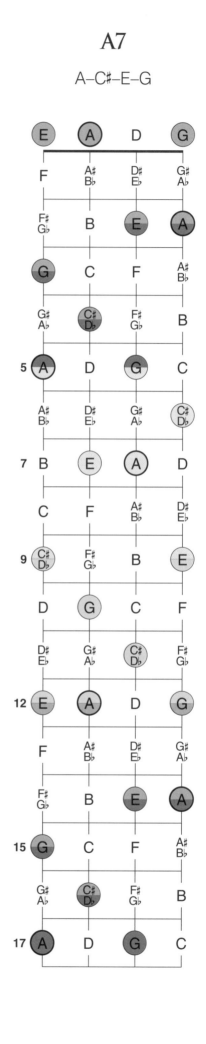

Bb7

Bb–D–F–Ab

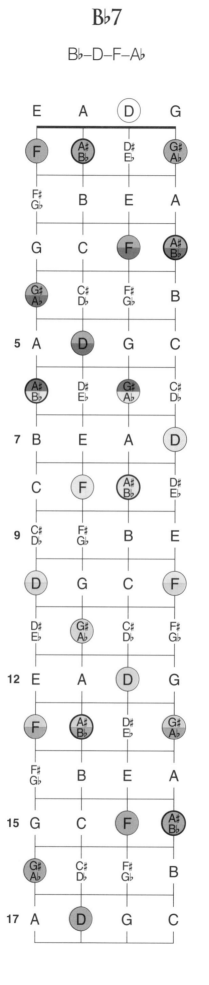

B7

B–D#–F#–A

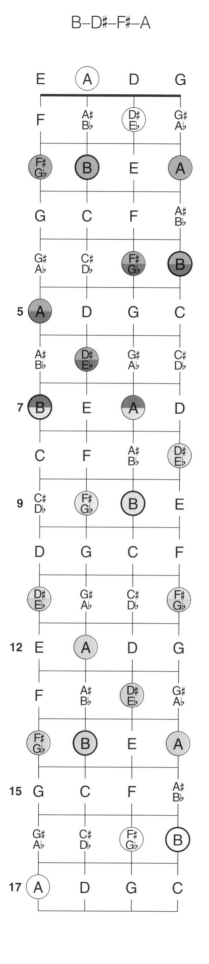

C7sus4

C–F–G–B♭

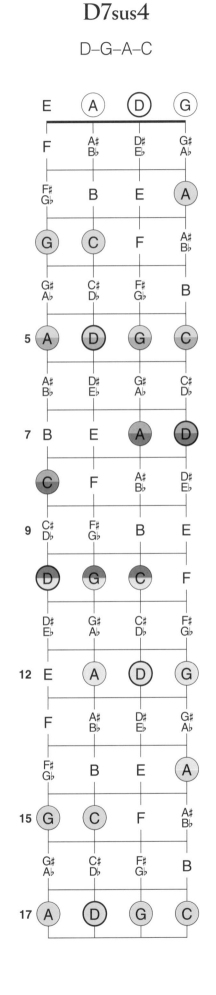

C#/D♭7sus4

C#–F#–G#–B/D♭–G♭–A♭–C♭

D7sus4

D–G–A–C

E♭7sus4

E♭–A♭–B♭–D♭

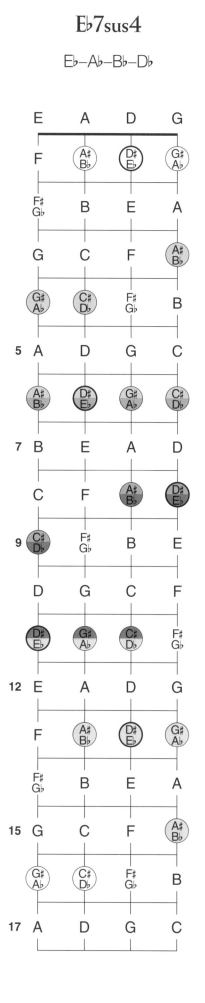

E7sus4

E–A–B–D

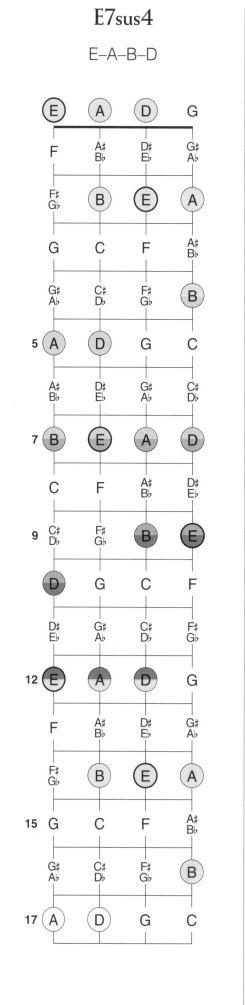

F7sus4

F–B♭–C–E♭

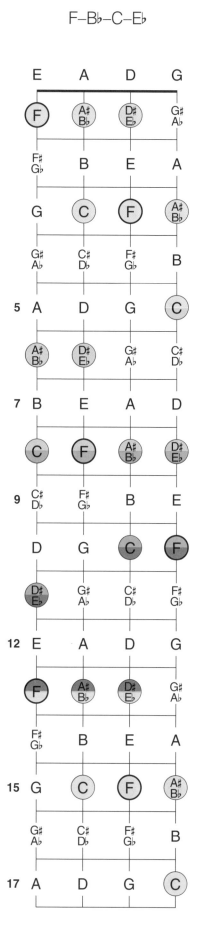

F#7sus4

F#–B–C#–E

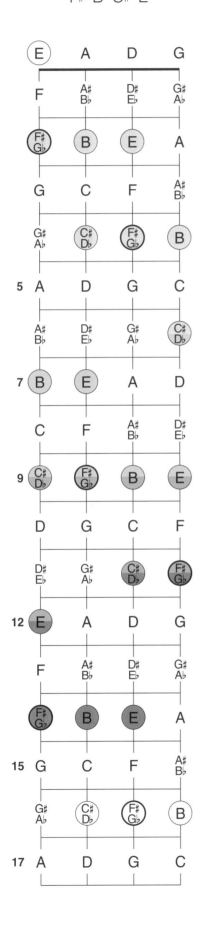

G7sus4

G–C–D–F

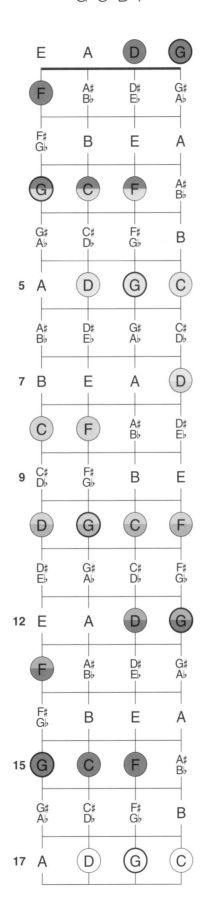

Ab7sus4

Ab–Db–Eb–Gb

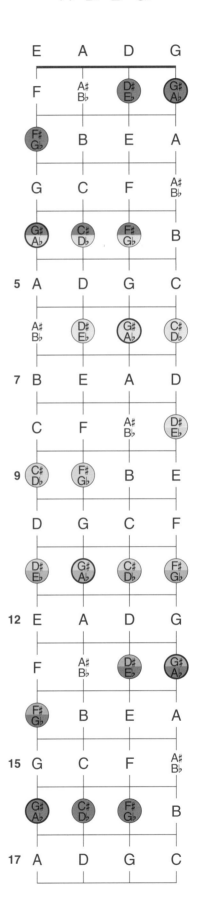

A7sus4

A–D–E–G

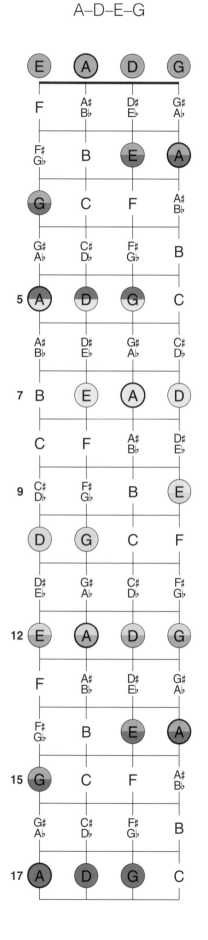

B♭7sus4

B♭–E♭–F–A♭

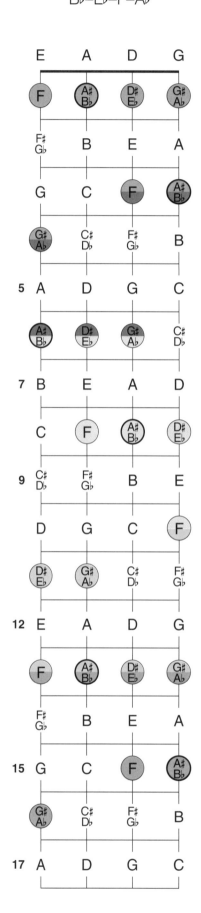

B7sus4

B–E–F♯–A

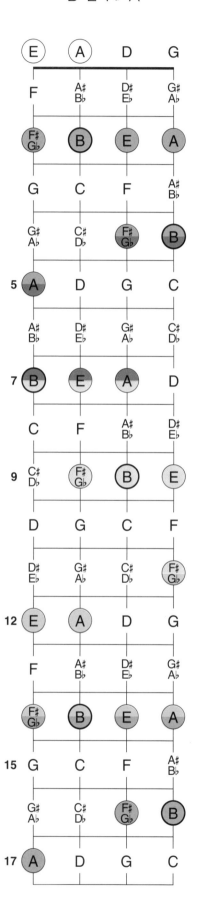

Cm7

C–E♭–G–B♭

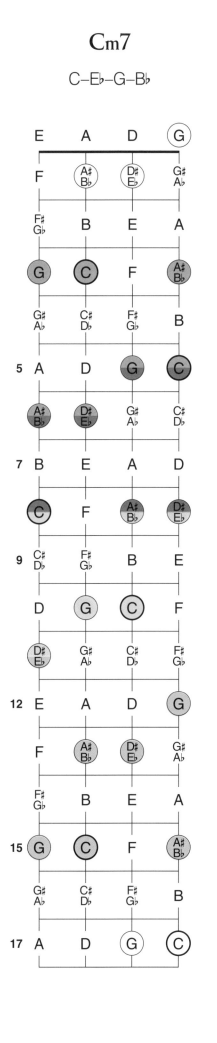

C#m7

C#–E–G#–B

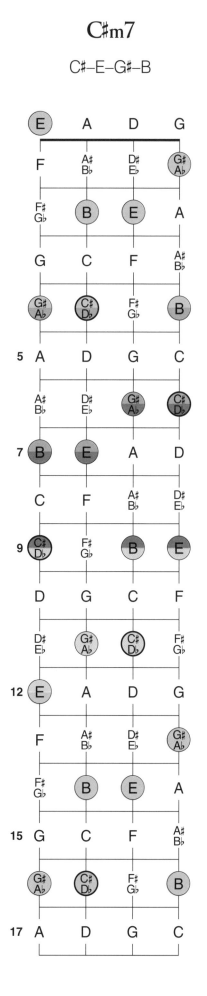

Dm7

D–F–A–C

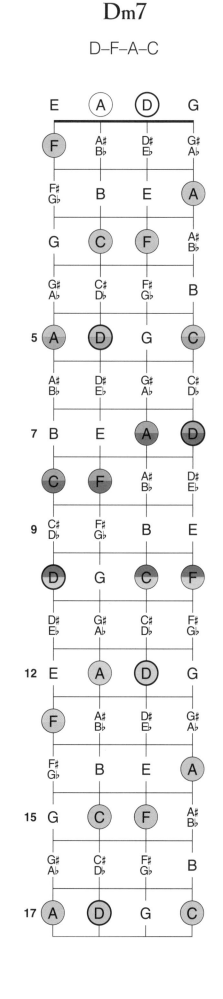

E♭m7

E♭–G♭–B♭–D♭

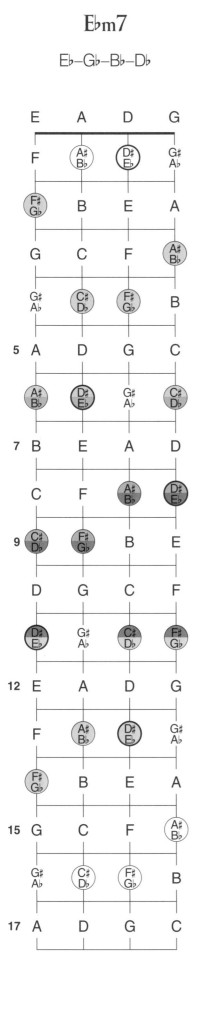

Em7

E–G–B–D

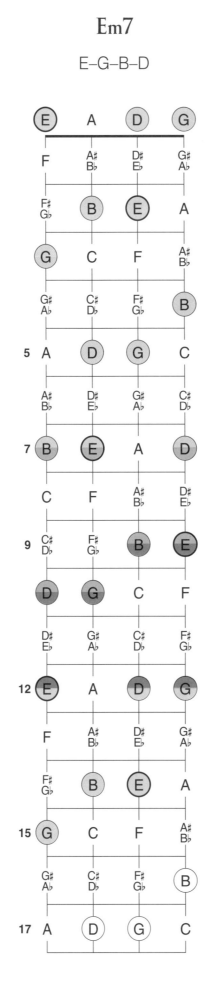

Fm7

F–A♭–C–E♭

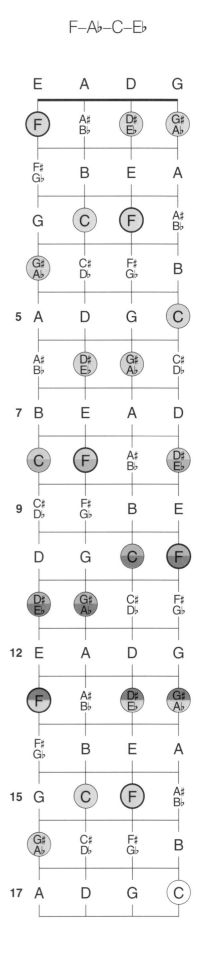

F#m7

F#–A–C#–E

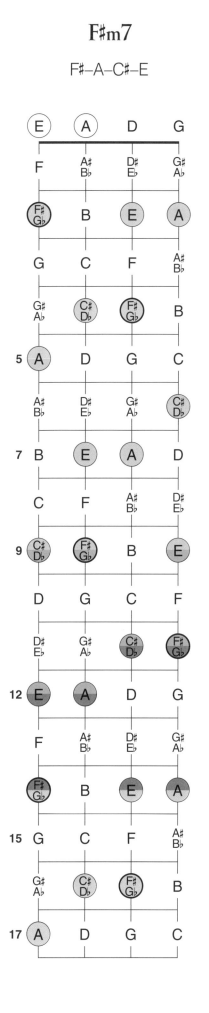

Gm7

G–B♭–D–F

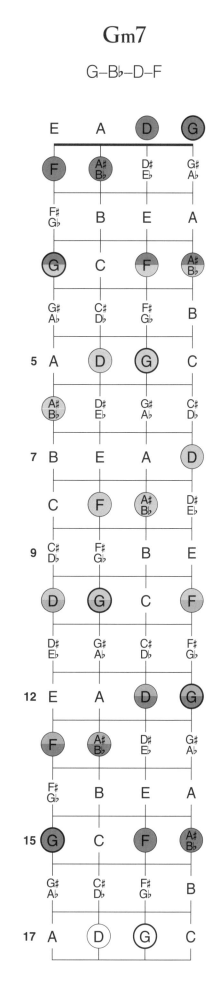

A♭m7

A♭–C♭–E♭–G♭

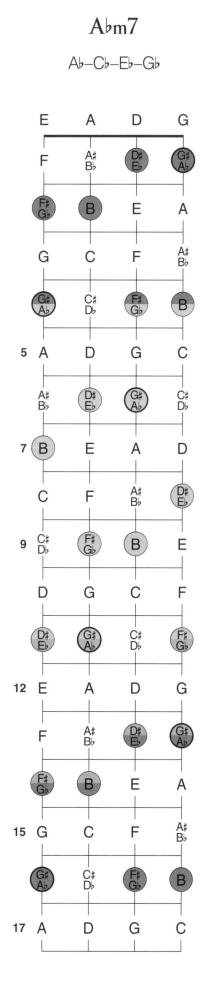

Am7

A–C–E–G

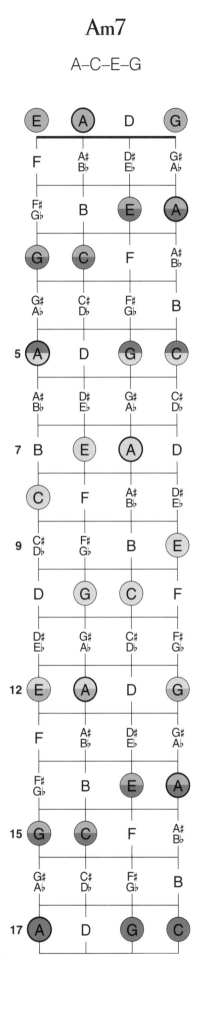

B♭m7

B♭–D♭–F–A♭

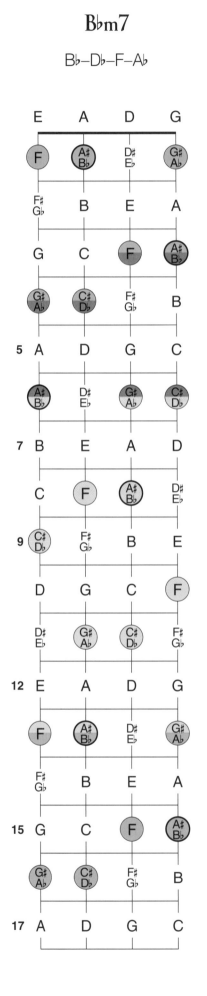

Bm7

B–D–F♯–A

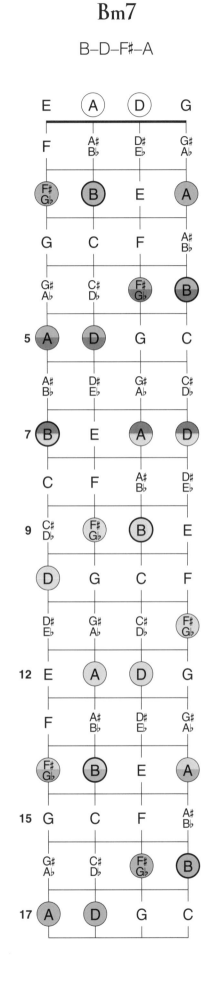

Cm(maj7)

C–E♭–G–B

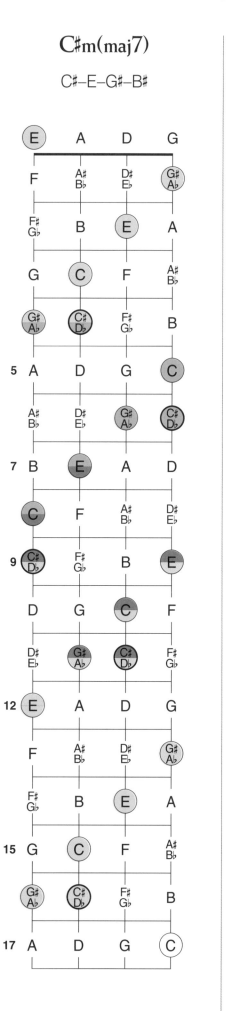

C♯m(maj7)

C♯–E–G♯–B♯

Dm(maj7)

D–F–A–C♯

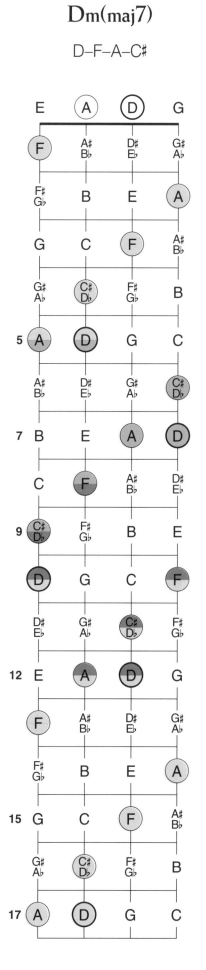

E♭m(maj7)

E♭–G♭–B♭–D

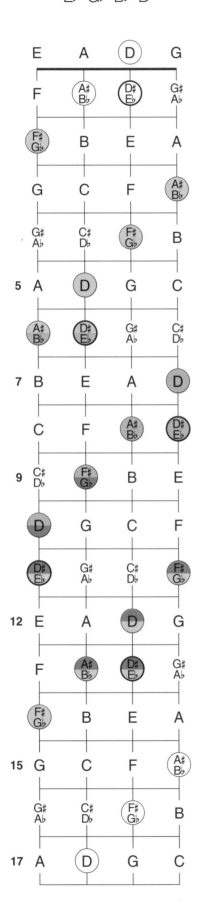

Em(maj7)

E–G–B–D♯

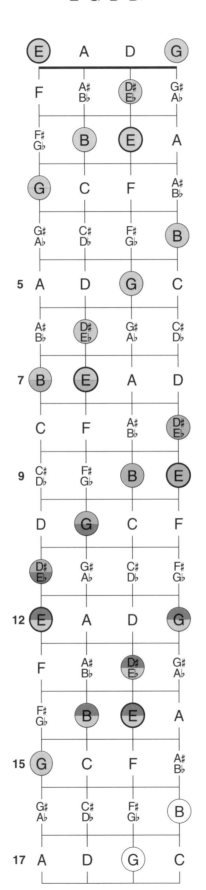

Fm(maj7)

F–A♭–C–E

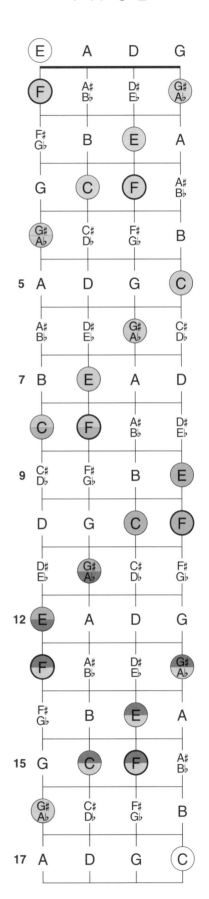

F#m(maj7)

F#–A–C#–E#

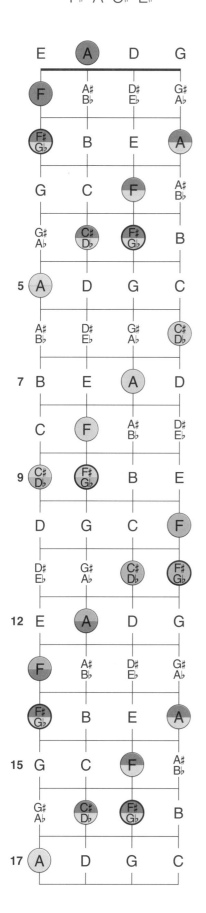

Gm(maj7)

G–Bb–D–F#

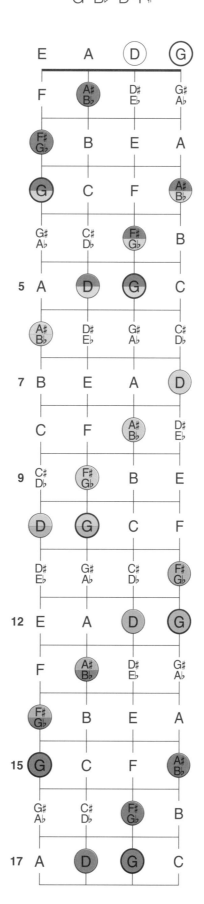

Abm(maj7)

Ab–Cb–Eb–G

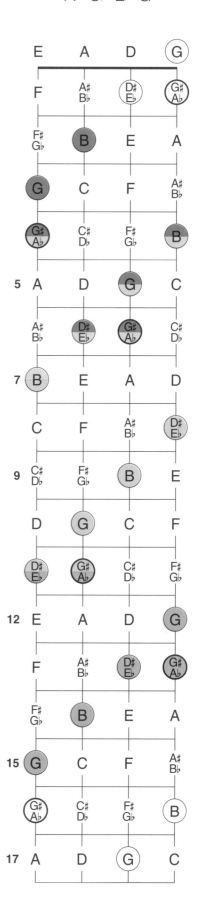

Am(maj7)

A–C–E–G♯

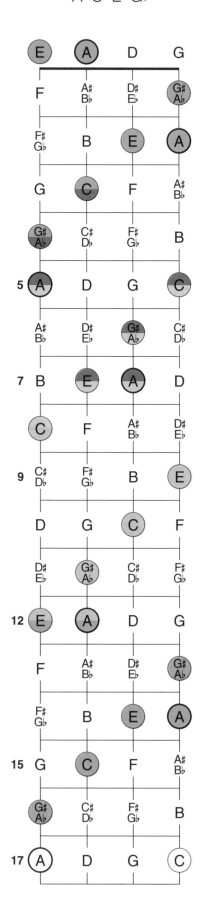

B♭m(maj7)

B♭–D♭–F–A

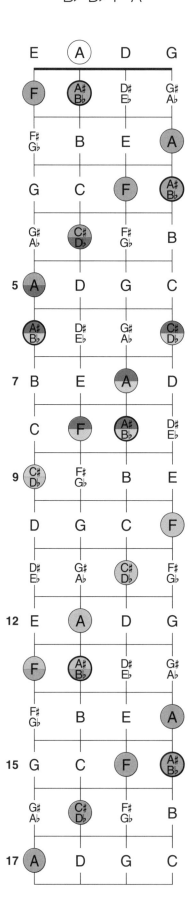

Bm(maj7)

B–D–F♯–A♯

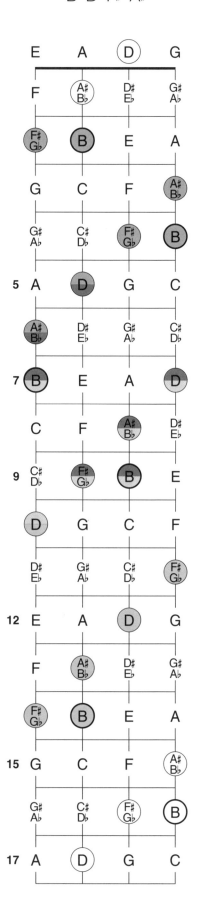

Cm7♭5

C–E♭–G♭–B♭

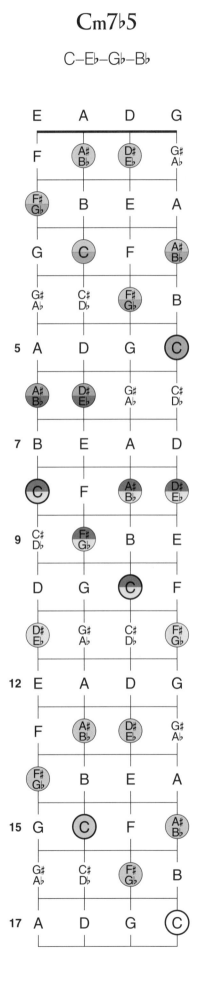

C#m7♭5

C#–E–G–B

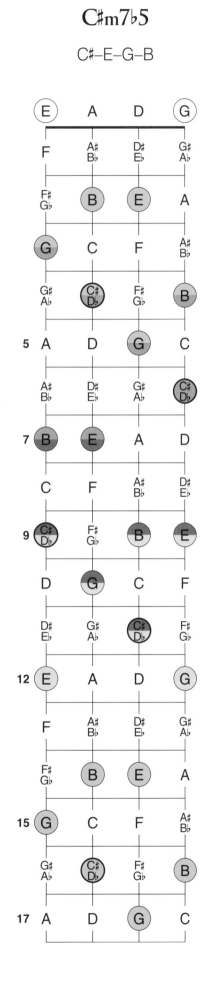

Dm7♭5

D–F–A♭–C

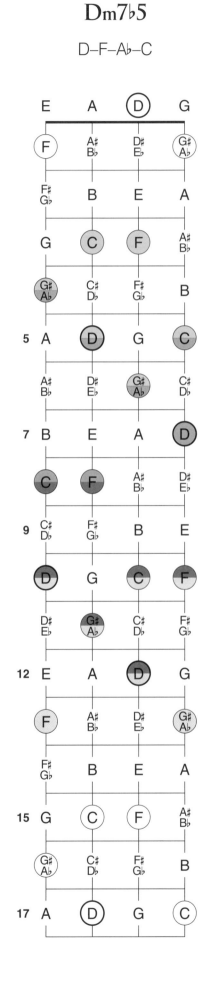

E♭m7♭5

E♭–G♭–B♭♭–D♭

Em7♭5

E–G–B♭–D

Fm7♭5

F–A♭–C♭–E♭

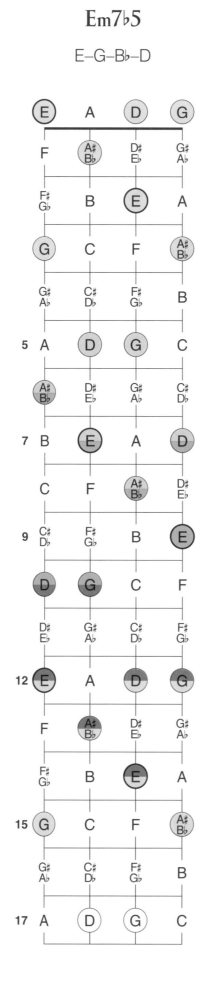

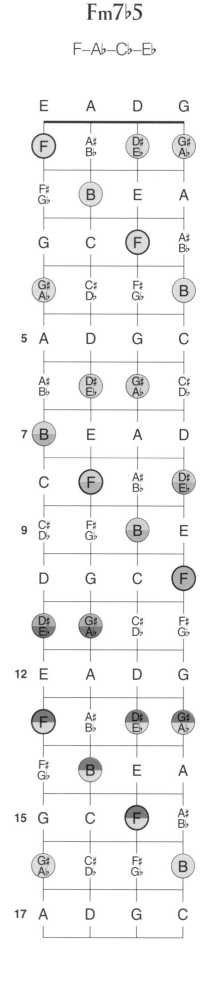

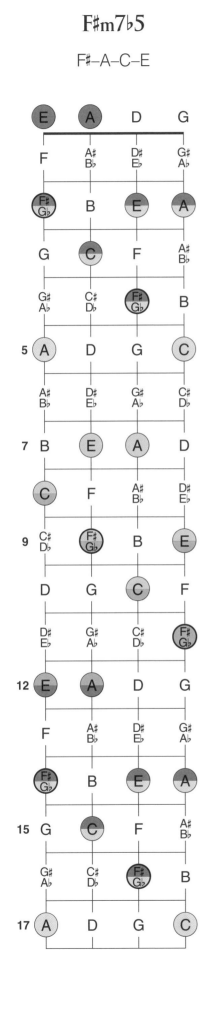

F#m7♭5

F#–A–C–E

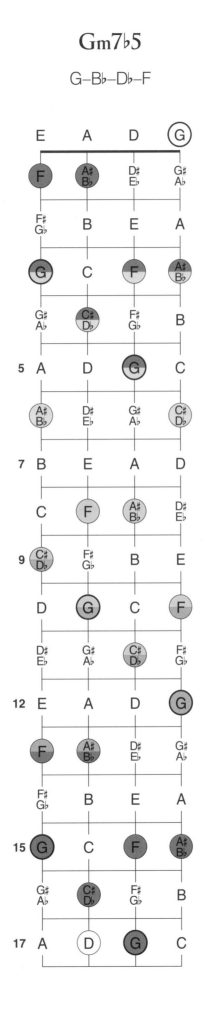

Gm7♭5

G–B♭–D♭–F

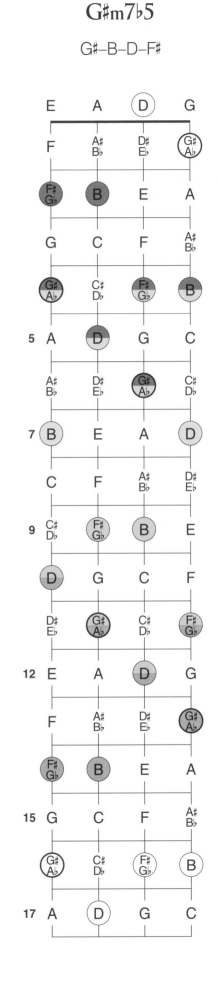

G#m7♭5

G#–B–D–F#

Am7♭5

A–C–E♭–G

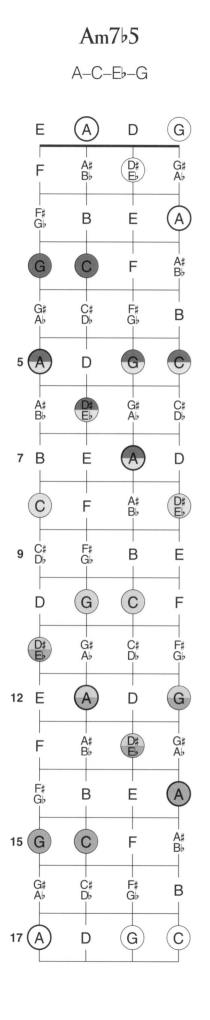

B♭m7♭5

B♭–D♭–F♭–A♭

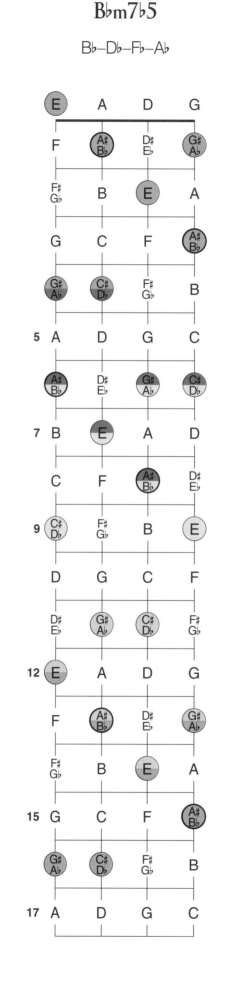

Bm7♭5

B–D–F–A

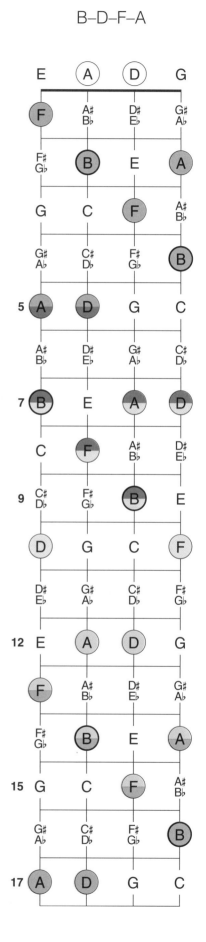

C°7

C–E♭–G♭–A

C#°7

C#–E–G–B♭

D°7

D–F–A♭–C♭

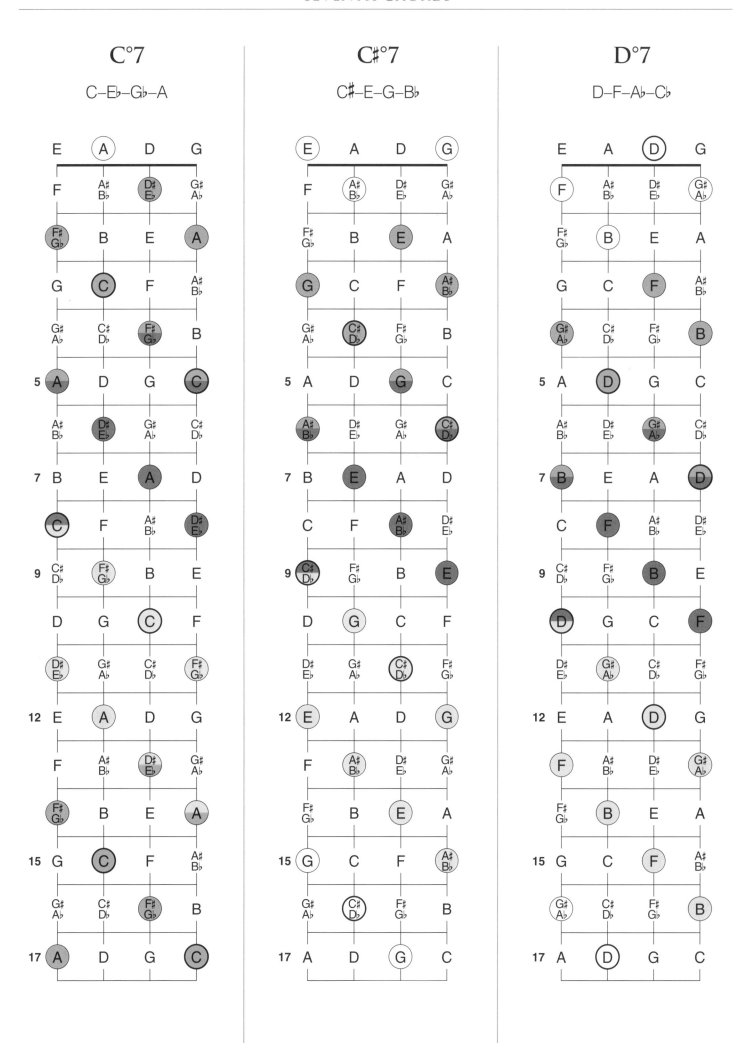

D♯°7

D♯–F♯–A–C

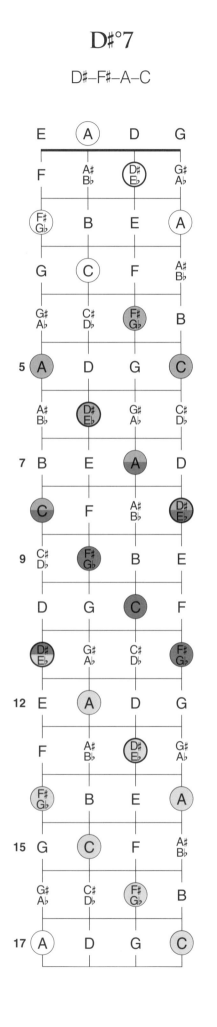

E°7

E–G–B♭–D♭

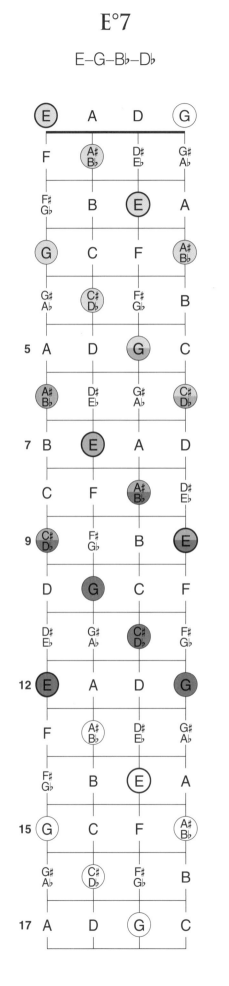

F°7

F–A♭–C♭–D

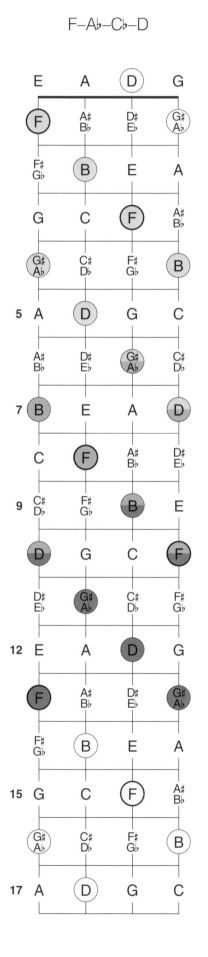

F#°7

F#–A–C–Eb

G°7

G–Bb–Db–Fb

G#°7

G#–B–D–F

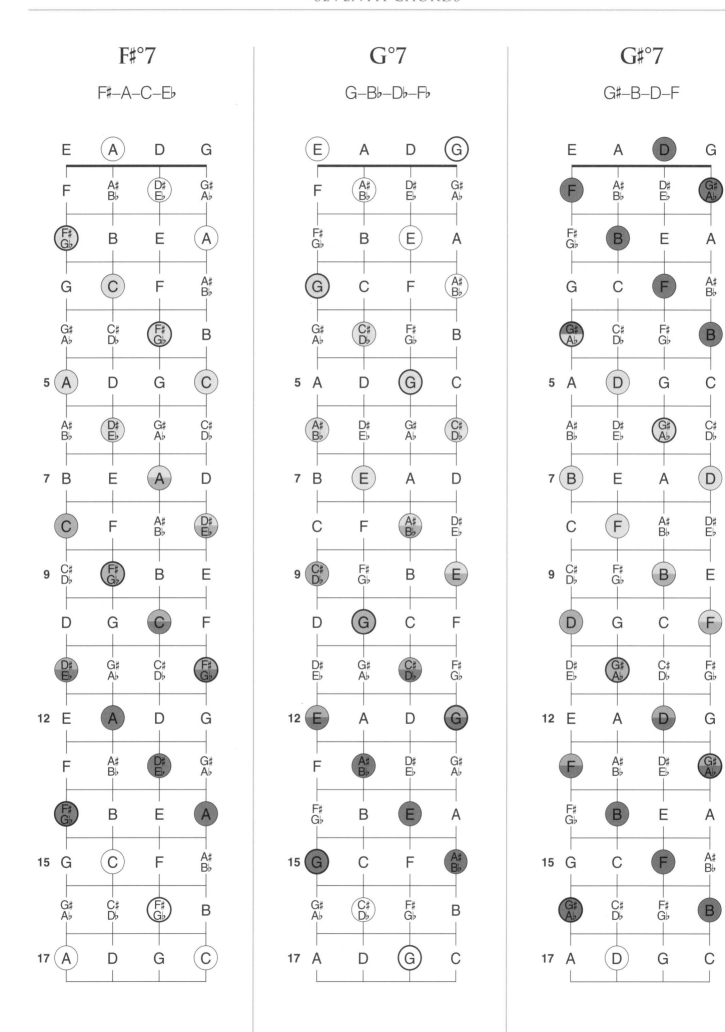

A°7

A–C–E♭–G♭

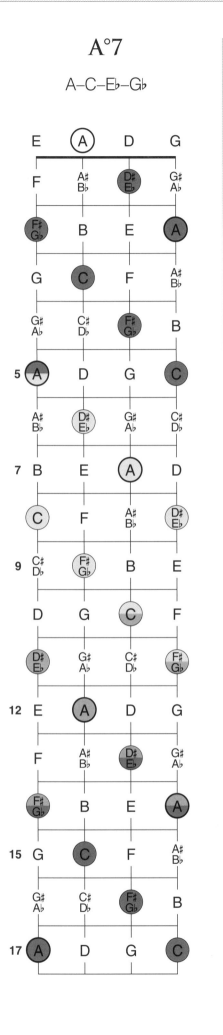

B♭°7

B♭–D♭–F♭–G

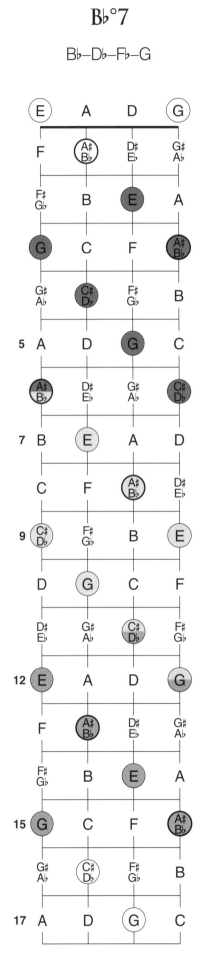

B°7

B–D–F–A♭

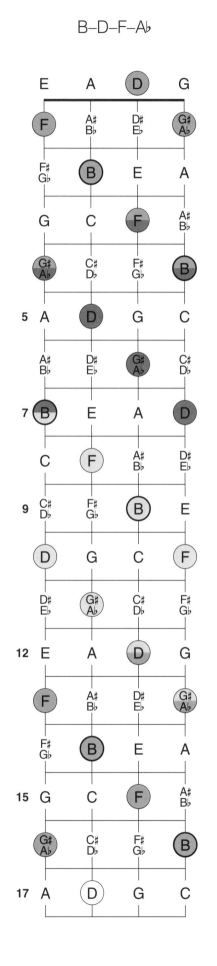